Bible Word Search

Volume II
Women in the Bible

GIL PUBLICATIONS
THE GOD IS LOVE MINISTRIES
P. O. Box 80275, Brooklyn, NY 11208
www.GILpublications.com
www.BibleWordSearchPuzzles.com

Bible Word Search
Volume II: Women in the Bible

Compiled by Akili Kumasi
Edited by Daisy Kumasi

ISBN: 0-9626035-3-8
ISBN 13: 978-0-9626035-3-2
Copyright © 2006 by GIL PUBLICATIONS
A division of THE GOD IS LOVE MINISTRIES

Scriptures marked (KJV) are taken from the King James Version of the Bible.

Scriptures marked (NIV) are taken from the New International Version of the Bible Scripture taken from the Holy Bible, NEW INTERNATIONAL VERSION®. Copyright © 1973, 1978, 1984 International Bible Society. All rights reserved throughout the world. Used by permission of International Bible Society. NEW INTERNATIONAL VERSION® and NIV® are registered trademarks of International Bible Society. Use of either trademark for the offering of goods or services requires the prior written consent of International Bible Society.

Versus marked (TLB) are taken from The Living Bible, copyright © 1971. Used by permission of Tyndale House Publishers, Inc., Wheaton Illinois 60189. All rights reserved.

Scripture quotations marked (NLT) are taken from the Holy Bible, New Living Translation, copyright © 1996. Used by permission of Tyndale House Publishers, Inc., Wheaton, Illinois 60189. All rights reserved.

Scripture marked NASB® are taken from the New American Standard Bible®. "Scripture quotations taken from the New American Standard Bible®, Copyright © 1960, 1962, 1963, 1968, 1971, 1972, 1973, 1975, 1977, 1995 by The Lockman Foundation. Used by permission." (www.Lockman.org)

Scripture marked AMP® are taken from the Amplified® Bible. Scripture quotations taken from the Amplified® Bible, Copyright © 1954, 1958, 1962, 1964, 1965, 1987 by The Lockman Foundation. Used by permission." (www.Lockman.org)

THIS IS A WITNESSING and BIBLE STUDY TOOL!
All parts of this book may be duplicated
for ministry, Godly teaching, witnessing and salvation purposes.
Permission to reproduce will be granted upon written request.

GIL PUBLICATIONS
THE GOD IS LOVE MINISTRIES
P. O. Box 80275, Brooklyn, NY 11208
info@GILpublications.com
www.GILpublications.com
www.BibleWordSearchPuzzles.com

Bible Word Search Volume II Women in the Bible

Introduction

Welcome to *Bible Word Search, Volume II: Women in the Bible.* This is the second in a series of *Bible Word Search* books. Eleven books are planned for this series. (See back of this book for more information)

Not only is this a fun book, but it also serves as a first-rate reference book with unparalleled information on the role of women in biblical times. God used many women to make contributions to His kingdom, but the enemy used some women too.

Unfortunately we were not able to put every woman who was mentioned in the Bible in *Bible Word Search, Volume II: Women in the Bible.* But, we believe that we have a good representation of significant women whose stories will greatly enhance your awareness of women's role, participation, and leadership.

For a more thorough treatment of women in the Bible we suggest you get a copy of *All the Women of the* Bible by Herbert Lockyer. This book was invaluable to us as we completed the research for *Bible Word Search, Volume II: Women in the Bible.* For more information on books on women in the Bible see the back of this book or go to our website on women in the Bible www.WomenInBible.com.

Bible Word Search, Volume II: Women in the Bible can be used is a variety of ways:

- Bible study groups
- Sunday school
- Personal enjoyment
- Biblical reference

Format of *Bible Word Search*

For each of the 80 topical themes (and 2 bonus topics) in this book, there is a selection of scriptures extracted from different translations of the Bible together with a word search puzzle that was made from the key words in the scriptures.

A list of the key words is located under the word search puzzle. The hidden key words in the puzzle can be forward, backward, upside down, right side up, horizontal, vertical or diagonally. Once you locate each word in the puzzle - circle it as shown on the back cover of this book and cross it off the list of key words.

We pray that you enjoy this book, can learn from it and are blessed by it.

Have some Godly fun!

Akili and Daisy Kumasi

Bible Word Search Volume II Women in the Bible

Table of Contents

Old Testament

1) A Virtuous Woman
2) Abigail
3) Bathsheba
4) Daughters of Men
5) Daughters of Zelophehad
6) Deborah
7) Delilah
8) Dinah
9) Esther
10) Eve
11) Great Woman of Shunem
12) Hagar
13) Hannah
14) Jael
15) Jephthah's Daughter
16) Jezebel
17) Jochebed, Moses' Mother
18) Leah
19) Lot's Wife and Daughters
20) Maid of Naaman's Wife
21) Michal
22) Miriam
23) Naomi

Bible Word Search, Vol. II: Women In the Bible

24) Pharaoh's Daughter
25) Potiphar's Wife
26) Proverbs: Women, Wives, Mothers
27) Queen of Sheba
28) Rachel
29) Rahab
30) Rebekak
31) Rizpah
32) Ruth
33) Samson's Mother
34) Sarah
35) Solomon's Wives
36) Tamar
37) Two Harlot Mothers (with Solomon)
38) Vashti
39) Widow of Zarephath
40) Widow's Oil
41) Wise Woman of Abel
42) Woman of Thebez
43) Woman with Familiar Spirit at Endor
44) Zipporah, Moses' Wife

New Testament

45) A Woman's Beauty is Measured By
46) Afflicted Daughter of Abraham
47) Anna, The Prophetess
48) Daughters of Jerusalem
49) Demon Possessed Damsel
50) Dorcas (Tabitha)
51) Elizabeth
52) Euodia and Syntche
53) Godly Wives
54) Herodias and the Beheading of John the Baptist
55) Jairus' Daughter
56) Jesus' Sisters

Bible Word Search, Vol. II: Women In the Bible

57) Lydia
58) Mary and Martha with Lazarus
59) Mary and Martha: Only One Thing is Needed
60) Mary Anoints Jesus,
    Woman with Alabaster Box
61) Mary Magdalene
62) Mary, Mother of James and Joses
63) Mary, Mother of Jesus
64) Mary, Mother of Mark John, with Rhoda
65) Persistent Widow
66) Peter's Mother-In-Law
67) Pheobe
68) Pilate's Wife
69) Priscilla
70) Salome, Mother of Zebedee's Children
71) Samarian Woman by Jacob's Well
72) Sapphira, Ananias' Wife
73) Spiritual Motherhood
74) Ten Virgins
75) Widow Who Gave Two Mites
76) Woman Caught In Adultery
77) Woman Who Begged for Daughter's Healing
78) Woman With the Issue of Blood
79) Women in Church
80) Women with Jesus

Two Bonus Puzzles
81) Aged and Young Women
82) Widows and Idle Women

Puzzle Solutions

GIL Publications Catalog

1. A Virtuous Woman

Who can find a <u>virtuous</u> woman? for her <u>price</u> is far above <u>rubies</u>.

The heart of her husband doth <u>safely</u> <u>trust</u> in her, so that he shall have no need of <u>spoil</u>.

She will do him good and not evil all the days of her life.

She <u>seek</u>eth <u>wool</u>, and <u>flax</u>, and worketh willingly with her hands.

She is like the merchants' ships; she bringeth her food from afar.

She <u>ris</u>eth also while it is yet night, and giveth meat to her household, and a portion to her maidens.

She <u>consider</u>eth a <u>field</u>, and <u>buy</u>eth it: with the fruit of her hands she <u>plant</u>eth a vineyard.

She girdeth her loins with strength, and strengtheneth her arms.

She perceiveth that her merchandise is good: her <u>candle</u> goeth not out by night.

She layeth her hands to the <u>spindle</u>, and her hands hold the distaff.

She stretcheth out her hand to the poor; yea, she <u>reach</u>eth forth her hands to the needy. She is not afraid of the <u>snow</u> for her household: for all her household are clothed with <u>scarlet</u>.

She maketh herself coverings of <u>tapestry</u>; her clothing is silk and purple. Her husband is known in the <u>gates</u>, when he sitteth among the elders of the land.

She maketh fine <u>linen</u>, and <u>sell</u>eth it; and delivereth girdles unto the merchant.

Strength and honour are her clothing; and she shall <u>rejoice</u> in time to come.

She <u>open</u>eth her mouth with wisdom; and in her <u>tongue</u> is the law of kindness.

She looketh well to the ways of her household, and eateth not the bread of idleness.

Her children arise up, and call her <u>blessed</u>; her husband also, and he praiseth her.

Many daughters have done virtuously, but thou excellest them all.

Favour is deceitful, and <u>beauty</u> is vain: but a woman that feareth the LORD, she shall be <u>praised</u>.

Give her of the fruit of her <u>hands</u>; and let her own works praise her in the gates. (Proverbs 31:10-31 KJV)

Bible Word Search, Vol. II: Women in the Bible

```
D L E I F E L D N I P S P T
G B E A U T Y N E P O R E Y
N L O O W W O N S C A L L E
P L A N T D I S O I R E C E
S S D N A H N N S A F I H C
U L I O P S S E C A R I S E
O T Q P Y I D S S P K E E S
U S A O D R D E R H B U Y X
T U C E L E T E C U C G S A
R R R I L S S S S I B A F L
I T N D E L E V E S O I E F
V E N T H V L G O P E J E R
N A A V B D L D X L A L E S
C G C H M E U G N O T T B R
```

Copyright © GIL PUBLICATIONS 2006

1. A Virtuous Woman

BEAUTY	OPEN	SEEK
BLESSED	PLANT	SELL
BUY	PRAISED	SNOW
CANDLE	PRICE	SPINDLE
CONSIDER	REACH	SPOIL
FIELD	REJOICE	TAPESTRY
FLAX	RISE	TONGUE
GATES	RUBIES	TRUST
HANDS	SAFELY	VIRTUOUS
LINEN	SCARLET	WOOL

GIL Publications, P. O. Box 80275, Brooklyn, NY 11208
www.BibleWordSearchPuzzles.com

2. Abigail

This man's name was <u>Nabal</u>, and his wife, <u>Abigail</u>, was a <u>sensible</u> and beautiful woman. But Nabal, a descendant of <u>Caleb</u>, was mean and dishonest in all his dealings.

When David heard that Nabal was <u>shearing</u> his <u>sheep</u>, he sent ten of his young men to <u>Carmel</u>.

Meanwhile, one of Nabal's servants went to Abigail and told her, "David sent men from the <u>wilderness</u> to talk to our master, and he insulted them. You'd better think fast, for there is going to be trouble for our master and his whole family. He's so ill-<u>tempered</u> that no one can even talk to him!"

Abigail lost no time. She quickly gathered two hundred <u>loaves</u> of <u>bread</u>, two <u>skins</u> of <u>wine</u>, five dressed sheep, nearly a bushel of roasted grain, one hundred <u>raisin</u> cakes, and two hundred <u>fig cakes</u>. She <u>packed</u> them on donkeys and said to her servants, "Go on ahead. I will follow you shortly." But she didn't tell her husband what she was doing.

When Abigail saw David, she quickly got off her donkey and <u>bowed</u> low before him. She fell at his feet and said, "I accept all <u>blame</u> in this matter, my lord. Please listen to what I have to say. I know Nabal is a wicked and ill-tempered man; please don't pay any attention to him. He is a <u>fool</u>, just as his name suggests. But I never even saw the messengers you sent."

David replied to Abigail, "Praise the LORD, the God of Israel, who has sent you to meet me today! Thank God for your good sense! Bless you for keeping me from murdering the man and carrying out <u>vengeance</u> with my own hands."

When Abigail arrived home, she found that Nabal had thrown a big <u>party</u> and was <u>celebrating</u> like a king. He was very drunk, so she didn't tell him anything about her meeting with David until the next morning. The next <u>morning</u> when he was sober, she told him what had happened. As a result he had a <u>stroke</u>, and he lay on his bed <u>paralyzed</u>. About ten days later, the LORD struck him and he died.

When David heard that Nabal was dead, he said, "Praise the LORD, who has <u>paid</u> back Nabal and kept me from doing it myself. Nabal has received the punishment for his sin." Then David wasted no time in sending messengers to Abigail to ask her to become his wife.

When the messengers arrived at Carmel, they told Abigail, "David has sent us to ask if you will marry him."

She bowed low to the ground and responded, "Yes, I am even willing to become a slave to David's servants!" Quickly getting ready, she took along five of her <u>servant</u> girls as <u>attendants</u>, mounted her <u>donkey</u>, and went with David's messengers. And so she became his wife.

(1 Samuel 25: 3-5, 14, 17-19, 23-25, 32-33, 36-42 NLT)

GIL Publications, P. O. Box 80275, Brooklyn, NY 11208
www.BibleWordSearchPuzzles.com

Bible Word Search, Vol. II: Women in the Bible

Copyright © GIL Publications 2006

2. Abigail

- ABIGAIL
- ATTENDANTS
- BLAME
- BOWED
- BREAD
- CAKES
- CALEB
- CARMEL
- CELEBRATING
- DONKEY
- FIG
- FOOL
- LOAVES
- MORNING
- NABAL
- PACKED
- PAID
- PARALYZED
- PARTY
- RAISIN
- SENSIBLE
- SERVANT
- SHEARING
- SHEEP
- SKINS
- STROKE
- TEMPERED
- VENGEANCE
- WILDERNESS
- WINE

GIL Publications, P. O. Box 80275, Brooklyn, NY 11208
www.BibleWordSearchPuzzles.com

3. Bathsheba

The following spring, the time of year when kings go to war, David sent Joab and the Israelite army to destroy the Ammonites. In the process they laid siege to the city of Rabbah. But David stayed behind ...
Late one afternoon David got out of bed after taking a nap and went for a stroll on the roof of the palace. As he looked out over the city, he noticed a woman of unusual beauty taking a bath. He sent someone to find out who she was, and he was told, "She is Bathsheba, the daughter of Eliam and the wife of Uriah the Hittite." Then David sent for her; and when she came to the palace, he slept with her. (She had just completed the purification rites after having her menstrual period.) Then she returned home. Later, when Bathsheba discovered that she was pregnant, she sent a message to inform David. (2 Samuel 11:1-5 NLT)

And he wrote in the letter, saying, Set ye Uriah in the forefront of the hottest battle, and retire ye from him, that he may be smitten, and die ...
And when the wife of Uriah heard that Uriah her husband was dead, she mourned for her husband.
And when the mourning was past, David sent and fetched her to his house, and she became his wife, and bare him a son. But the thing that David had done displeased the LORD. (2 Samuel 11:15, 26-27 KJV)

Howbeit, because by this deed thou hast given great occasion to the enemies of the LORD to blaspheme, the child also that is born unto thee shall surely die ... And David comforted Bathsheba his wife, and went in unto her, and lay with her: and she bare a son, and he called his name Solomon: and the LORD loved him. (2 Samuel 12:14, 24 KJV) .

So Bathsheba went to see the aged king in his room ... bowed low and knelt before the king. "My lord, you yourself swore to me your servant by the LORD your God: 'Solomon your son shall be king after me, and he will sit on my throne.' But now Adonijah has become king, and you, my lord the king, do not know about it ... the eyes of all Israel are on you, to learn from you who will sit on the throne of my lord the king after him.
... The king then took an oath: "As surely as the LORD lives, who has delivered me out of every trouble, I will surely carry out today what I swore to you by the LORD, the God of Israel: Solomon your son shall be king after me, and he will sit on my throne in my place." (1 King 1:15-21, 28-30 NIV)

Bible Word Search, Vol. II: Women in the Bible

```
I P X B A T T L E P T V A V P
H A H T A B D E B S H B B L C
G N I R P S I L R A R A Q S D
S E T I R O S I N F O R M I N
E G E I S L P A O O N E C T D
G B R P H O L M O O E T G Q A
A A A A A M E D N R A I V B G
S O W L B O A A R J B U G S H
S J U A B N S V E L E N A K G
E A R C A R E I T L H U B Z B
M R I E R P D D F O S S Y Q Z
Y M A W O A T H A R H U I P B
G Y H I T T I T E T T A Q D C
T A D O N I J A H S A L N J L
B L A S P H E M E Y B R E O I
```

COPYRIGHT © GIL PUBLICATIONS 2006

3. Bathsheba

ADONIJAH	DISPLEASED	RITES
AFTERNOON	ELIAM	ROOF
ARMY	HITTITE	SIEGE
BARE	INFORM	SOLOMON
BATH	JOAB	SPRING
BATHSHEBA	MESSAGE	STROLL
BATTLE	NAP	THRONE
BED	OATH	UNUSUAL
BLASPHEME	PALACE	URIAH
DAVID	RABBAH	WAR

GIL Publications, P. O. Box 80275, Brooklyn, NY 11208
www.BibleWordSearchPuzzles.com

4. Daughters of Men

Genesis 6:1-4

And it came to pass, when men began to <u>multiply</u> on the <u>face</u> of the <u>earth</u>, and <u>daughters</u> were <u>born</u> unto them, That the sons of God saw the daughters of men that they *were* <u>fair</u>; and they took them wives of all which they chose.

And the LORD said, My spirit shall not always <u>strive</u> with man, for that he also *is* <u>flesh</u>: yet his days shall be an <u>hundred</u> and <u>twenty</u> years.

There were <u>giants</u> in the earth in those days; and also after that, when the sons of God came in unto the daughters of men, and they bare *children* to them, the same *became* <u>mighty</u> men which *were* of old, men of <u>renown</u>. (KJV)

When men began to <u>increase</u> in <u>number</u> on the earth and daughters were born to them, the sons of God saw that the daughters of men were <u>beautiful</u>, and they married any of them they <u>chose</u>. Then the LORD said, "My Spirit will not <u>contend</u> with man forever, for he is <u>mortal</u>; his days will be a hundred and twenty years."

The <u>Nephilim</u> were on the earth in those days—and also <u>afterward</u>—when the sons of God went to the daughters of men and had children by them. They were the <u>heroes</u> of old, men of renown. (NIV)

When the human <u>population</u> began to <u>grow</u> <u>rapidly</u> on the earth, the sons of God saw the beautiful women of the <u>human</u> <u>race</u> and took any they wanted as their wives. Then the LORD said, "My Spirit will not put up with humans for such a long time, for they are only mortal flesh. In the <u>future</u>, they will live no more than 120 years."

In those days, and even afterward, giants lived on the earth, for whenever the sons of God had intercourse with human women, they gave birth to children who became the heroes <u>mentioned</u> in <u>legends</u> of old. (NLT)

4. Daughters of Men

AFTERWARD	FUTURE	MORTAL
BEAUTIFUL	GIANTS	MULTIPLY
BORN	GROW	NEPHILIM
CHOSE	HEROES	NUMBER
CONTEND	HUMAN	POPULATION
DAUGHTERS	HUNDRED	RACE
EARTH	INCREASE	RAPIDLY
FACE	LEGENDS	RENOWN
FAIR	MENTIONED	STRIVE
FLESH	MIGHTY	TWENTY

5. Daughters of Zelophehad

The <u>daughters</u> of <u>Zelophehad</u> son of <u>Hepher</u>, the son of <u>Gilead</u>, the son of <u>Makir</u>, the son of <u>Manasseh</u>, belonged to the <u>clans</u> of Manasseh son of <u>Joseph</u>. The names of the daughters were <u>Mahlah</u>, <u>Noah</u>, <u>Hoglah</u>, <u>Milcah</u> and <u>Tirzah</u>. They approached the entrance to the <u>Tent</u> of <u>Meeting</u> and stood before Moses, Eleazar the <u>priest</u>, the leaders and the whole <u>assembly</u>, and said, "Our father died in the desert. He was not among <u>Korah</u>'s followers, who <u>banded</u> together against the LORD, but he died for his own sin and left no sons. Why should our father's name disappear from his clan because he had no son? Give us <u>property</u> among our father's relatives."

So Moses brought their <u>case</u> before the LORD and the LORD said to him, "What Zelophehad's daughters are saying is right. You must <u>certainly</u> give them property as an <u>inheritance</u> among their father's relatives and <u>turn</u> their father's inheritance over to them.

"Say to the Israelites, 'If a man dies and <u>leaves</u> no son, turn his inheritance over to his daughter. If he has no daughter, give his inheritance to his brothers. If he has no brothers, give his inheritance to his father's brothers. If his father had no brothers, give his inheritance to the <u>nearest</u> relative in his clan, that he may <u>possess</u> it. This is to be a <u>legal</u> requirement for the <u>Israelites</u>, as the LORD <u>commanded</u> Moses.'" (Numbers 27:1-11 NIV)

Bible Word Search, Vol. II: Women in the Bible

```
I H E P H E R G F T G I E O O
J A T T I R Z A H A O N S R G
C C G G I L E A D D K H R C H
C L N K L A L G N I T E E M C
E I A E Z H O G L A H R T T E
B M G N A B P B T G S I H S R
W A K M S R H A R O K T G E T
L N N Y T R E P O R P A U I A
E A J D Q O H S E M S N A R I
A S N N E R A V T S G C D P N
V S O F S D D I E P O E G G L
E E T A A P P M F D C J X B Y
S H Y N C Q B P O S S E S S V
I S R A E L I T E S Z W H E G
O B Y C Y T D E D N A M M O C
```

COPYRIGHT © GIL PUBLICATIONS 2006

5. Daughters of Zelophehad

ASSEMBLY	INHERITANCE	MILCAH
BANDED	ISRAELITES	NEAREST
CASE	JOSEPH	NOAH
CERTAINLY	KORAH	POSSESS
CLANS	LEAVES	PRIEST
COMMANDED	LEGAL	PROPERTY
DAUGHTERS	MAHLAH	TENT
GILEAD	MAKIR	TIRZAH
HEPHER	MANASSEH	TURN
HOGLAH	MEETING	ZELOPHEHAD

GIL Publications, P. O. Box 80275, Brooklyn, NY 11208
www.BibleWordSearchPuzzles.com

6. Deborah

And the children of Israel again did <u>evil</u> in the <u>sight</u> of the LORD, when <u>Ehud</u> was dead.

And the LORD sold them into the hand of <u>Jabin</u> king of Canaan, that <u>reigned</u> in <u>Hazor</u>; the <u>captain</u> of whose <u>host</u> was <u>Sisera</u>, which <u>dwelt</u> in Harosheth of the <u>Gentiles</u>.

And the children of Israel cried unto the LORD: for he had <u>nine</u> hundred <u>chariots</u> of <u>iron</u>; and <u>twenty</u> years he mightily <u>oppressed</u> the children of Israel.

And <u>Deborah</u>, a <u>prophetess</u>, the wife of <u>Lapidoth</u>, she <u>judged</u> Israel at that time. And she dwelt under the <u>palm</u> tree of Deborah between Ramah and <u>Bethel</u> in mount Ephraim: and the children of Israel came up to her for judgment.

And she sent and called <u>Barak</u> the son of Abinoam out of Kedeshnaphtali, and said unto him, Hath not the LORD God of Israel commanded, saying, Go and draw toward mount <u>Tabor</u>, and take with thee ten thousand men of the children of <u>Naphtali</u> and of the children of <u>Zebulun</u>?

And I will draw unto thee to the river Kishon Sisera, the captain of Jabin's army, with his chariots and his multitude; and I will deliver him into thine hand.

And Barak said unto her, If thou wilt go with me, then I will go: but if thou wilt not go with me, then I will not go.

And she said, I will surely go with thee: notwithstanding the journey that thou takest shall not be for thine <u>honour</u>; for the LORD shall sell Sisera into the hand of a woman. And Deborah arose, and went with Barak to Kedesh.

And Barak called Zebulun and Naphtali to Kedesh; and he went up with ten thousand men at his feet: and Deborah went up with him.

And Deborah said unto Barak, Up; for this is the day in which the LORD hath delivered Sisera into thine hand: is not the LORD gone out before thee? So Barak went down from mount Tabor, and <u>ten</u> thousand men after him.

Then sang Deborah and Barak the son of Abinoam on that day, saying, Praise ye the LORD for the avenging of Israel, when the people <u>willingly</u> offered themselves. (Judges 4:1-10, 14; 5:1-2 KJV)

Bible Word Search, Vol. II: Women in the Bible

```
K O N I A T P A C O G A L N N
V Y I Z D W E L T H G I S X W
F A D A D E S S E R P P O W W
G S U K E N H O N O U R H I Z
B I N A U T D P T N U O M L D
N S T R M Y H T O D I P A L H
D E G A L I B R O Z A H W I Z
I R O B A T N U L U B E Z N O
S A E S P C H A R I O T S G K
J A B I N W H A R O B E D L Z
K X S T G E N T I L E S E Y W
V S R Z B N V E R M T S O H E
I S J U D G E D O E H U D L N
L B S X Q E X D N H E N I N N
L K L K N A P H T A L I V E K
```

COPYRIGHT © GIL PUBLICATIONS 2006

6. Deborah

BARAK	HONOUR	PALM
BETHEL	HOST	PROPHETESS
CAPTAIN	IRON	REIGNED
CHARIOTS	JABIN	SIGHT
DEBORAH	JUDGED	SISERA
DWELT	LAPIDOTH	TABOR
EHUD	MOUNT	TEN
EVIL	NAPHTALI	TWENTY
GENTILES	NINE	WILLINGLY
HAZOR	OPPRESSED	ZEBULUN

GIL Publications, P. O. Box 80275, Brooklyn, NY 11208
www.BibleWordSearchPuzzles.com

7. Delilah

Some time later, he fell in love with a woman in the <u>Valley</u> of <u>Sorek</u> whose name was Delilah. The rulers of the <u>Philistines</u> went to her and said, "See if you can lure him into showing you the <u>secret</u> of his great strength and how we can <u>overpower</u> him so we may tie him up and subdue him. Each one of us will give you eleven hundred <u>shekels</u> of <u>silver</u>."

So <u>Delilah</u> said to <u>Samson</u>, "Tell me the secret of your great strength and how you can be tied up and subdued."

Samson answered her, "If anyone ties me with seven fresh <u>thongs</u> that have not been <u>dried</u>, I'll become as weak as any other man."

Then the rulers of the Philistines brought her seven fresh thongs that had not been dried, and she tied him with them. With men <u>hidden</u> in the room, she called to him, "Samson, the Philistines are upon you!" But he <u>snapped</u> the thongs as easily as a piece of <u>string</u> snaps when it comes close to a <u>flame</u>. So the secret of his strength was not discovered.

Then Delilah said to Samson, "You have made a fool of me; you <u>lied</u> to me. Come now, tell me how you can be tied."

He said, "If anyone ties me securely with new <u>ropes</u> that have never been used, I'll become as <u>weak</u> as any other man."

So Delilah took new ropes and tied him with them. Then, with men hidden in the room, she called to him, "Samson, the Philistines are upon you!" But he snapped the ropes off his arms as if they were <u>threads</u>.

Delilah then said to Samson, "Until now, you have been making a fool of me and lying to me. Tell me how you can be tied."

He replied, "If you weave the seven <u>braids</u> of my head into the <u>fabric</u> on the <u>loom</u> and <u>tighten</u> it with the pin, I'll become as weak as any other man." So while he was sleeping, Delilah took the seven braids of his head, <u>wove</u> them into the fabric and tightened it with the pin.

Again she called to him, "Samson, the Philistines are upon you!" He awoke from his sleep and pulled up the pin and the loom, with the fabric.

Then she said to him, "How can you say, 'I love you,' when you won't <u>confide</u> in me? This is the third time you have made a fool of me ..." With such <u>nagging</u> she <u>prodded</u> him day after day until he was tired to death.

So he told her everything. "No <u>razor</u> has ever been used on my head," he said, "because I have been a Nazirite set apart to God since birth. If my head were <u>shaved</u>, my strength would leave me ..."

When Delilah saw that he had told her everything, she sent word to the rulers of the Philistines, "Come back once more; he has told me everything." So the rulers of the Philistines returned with the silver in their hands. Having put him to sleep on her lap, she called a man to shave off the seven braids of his hair, and so began to <u>subdue</u> him. And his strength left him. (Judges 16:4-20 NIV)

Bible Word Search, Vol. II: Women in the Bible

```
H A L I L E D K R O P E S W S
T I G H T E N E J H I D D E N
N W X Y C Y W W I Y F I I A A
L F X G M O O L E L W F A K P
X E G T P V I L A W A N R N P
L S D R E S L M D B S O B R E
P Y E E T A E N R W U C O A D
C V Y I V X Z I I G B D K Z L
O Y N P Z A C L E Q D U I O O
B E T M T J H B D E U B T R Q
S A M S O N G S D A E R H T O
G W Y Y O Q R H Y E T O O A S
S I L V E R S T S T R I N G O
I Y T E R C E S G N I G G A N
P R Z Z S L E K E H S B S L G
```

COPYRIGHT © GIL PUBLICATIONS 2006

7. Delilah

BRAIDS	OVERPOWER	SNAPPED
CONFIDE	PHILISTINES	SOREK
DELILAH	PRODDED	STRING
DRIED	RAZOR	SUBDUE
FABRIC	ROPES	THONGS
FLAME	SAMSON	THREADS
HIDDEN	SECRET	TIGHTEN
LIED	SHAVED	VALLEY
LOOM	SHEKELS	WEAK
NAGGING	SILVER	WOVE

GIL Publications, P. O. Box 80275, Brooklyn, NY 11208
www.BibleWordSearchPuzzles.com

8. Dinah

Now Dinah, the daughter Leah had borne to Jacob, went out to visit the women of the land. When Shechem son of Hamor the Hivite, the ruler of that area, saw her, he took her and violated her. His heart was drawn to Dinah daughter of Jacob, and he loved the girl and spoke tenderly to her. And Shechem said to his father Hamor, "Get me this girl as my wife."

When Jacob heard that his daughter Dinah had been defiled, his sons were in the fields with his livestock; so he kept quiet about it until they came home.

Then Shechem said to Dinah's father and brothers, "Let me find favor in your eyes, and I will give you whatever you ask. Make the price for the bride and the gift I am to bring as great as you like, and I'll pay whatever you ask me. Only give me the girl as my wife."

Because their sister Dinah had been defiled, Jacob's sons replied deceitfully as they spoke to Shechem and his father Hamor.

Simeon and Levi, Dinah's brothers, took their swords and attacked the unsuspecting city, killing every male. They put Hamor and his son Shechem to the sword and took Dinah from Shechem's house and left. (Genesis 34:1-5, 11-13, 25-26 NIV)

Bible Word Search, Vol. II: Women in the Bible

8. Dinah

- ATTACKED
- BORNE
- BROTHERS
- DAUGHTER
- DECEITFULLY
- DEFILED
- DINAH
- DRAWN
- FIELDS
- GIRL
- HAMOR
- HEART
- JACOB
- KILLING
- LAND
- LEAH
- LEVI
- LIKE
- LIVESTOCK
- LOVED
- PAY
- PRICE
- RULER
- SHECHEM
- SIMEON
- SWORD
- TENDERLY
- VIOLATED
- WIFE
- WOMEN

9. Esther

[H]is attendants suggested, "Let us search the empire to find beautiful young virgins for the king ... who pleases you most will be made queen..." At the fortress of Susa there was a certain Jew named Mordecai ... had a beautiful and lovely young cousin, Hadassah ... (Esther) ... father and mother had died, Mordecai adopted her ... raised her as his own daughter ... the king loved her more than any of the other young women ... set the royal crown on her head and declared her queen instead of Vashti ... Esther continued to keep her nationality and family background a secret ... following Mordecai's orders...

... two of the king's eunuchs ... guards ... became angry at King Xerxes and plotted to assassinate him ... Mordecai heard about the plot and passed the information on to Queen Esther. She then told the king ... the two men were hanged on a gallows. (Esther 2: 2, 4, 5-7, 16-17, 20, 21-23 NLT)

Haman approached King Xerxes, "...If it please Your Majesty, issue a decree that they [Jews] be destroyed ... I will give 375 tons of silver to ... government administrators ... the royal treasury." (Esther 3: 6,8a, 9 NLT)

Mordecai [told Esther] "Do not think that because you are in the king's house you alone of all the Jews will escape ... Esther [replied] ... "... gather together all the Jews ... in Susa ... fast for me ... for three days ... I and my maids will fast as you do. [then] I will go to the king, even though it is against the law. And if I perish, I perish." (Esther 4:7, 13, 15-16 NIV)

[Esther said to the king] "If it pleases the king ... together with Haman, come today to a banquet I have prepared ..." [Haman's] wife Zeresh and all his friends said to him, "Have a gallows built, seventy-five feet high, and ask the king ... to have Mordecai hanged on it. Then go with the king to the dinner and be happy." ... Haman ... had the gallows built. (Esther 5:4, 14 NIV)

That night the king could not sleep; so he ordered the book of the chronicles, the record of his reign, to be brought in and read to him. It was found recorded there that Mordecai had exposed Bigthana and Teresh ... who had conspired to assassinate King Xerxes. (Esther 6:1-2 NIV)

Esther ... "If I have found favor with you, O king, and if it pleases your majesty, grant me my life—this is my petition ... spare my people ...[who] have been sold for destruction and slaughter and annihilation ..."

King Xerxes asked Queen Esther, "... Where is the man who has dared to do such a thing?" Esther said, "The adversary and enemy is this vile Haman."

... Haman was terrified ... The king got up in a rage ... [Haman] beg Queen Esther for his life ... king said, "Hang him ..." ... on the gallows ... prepared for Mordecai ... king's fury subsided. (Esther 7: 3-7, 9-10 NIV)

... King Xerxes gave Queen Esther the estate of Haman ... The king took off his signet ring ... reclaimed from Haman, and presented it to Mordecai. And Esther appointed him over Haman's estate. (Esther 8:1-2 NIV)

Bible Word Search, Vol. II: Women in the Bible

9. Esther

- ADVERSARY
- BANQUET
- BIGTHANA
- CROWN
- ENEMY
- ESTATE
- ESTHER
- EUNUCHS
- FORTRESS
- FURY
- GALLOWS
- HADASSAH
- HAMAN
- HANGED
- MAJESTY
- MORDECAI
- PERISH
- PETITION
- PLOTTED
- SECRET
- SIGNET
- SILVER
- SLAUGHTER
- SUSA
- TERESH
- TREASURY
- VASHTI
- VILE
- XERXES
- ZERESH

GIL Publications, P. O. Box 80275, Brooklyn, NY 11208
www.BibleWordSearchPuzzles.com

10. Eve

So God created man in his own image, in the <u>image</u> of God he created him; male and <u>female</u> he created them. God blessed them and said to them, "Be <u>fruitful</u> and increase in number; fill the earth and subdue it.

The LORD God said, "It is not good for the man to be alone. I will make a <u>helper</u> <u>suitable</u> for him

So the LORD God caused the man to fall into a deep <u>sleep</u> ... he took one of the man's ribs ... made a <u>woman</u> from the <u>rib</u> ... and he brought her to the man. The man said, "This is now <u>bone</u> of my bones and <u>flesh</u> of my flesh; she shall be called 'woman, 'for she was <u>taken</u> out of man."

For this reason a man will leave his father and mother and be united to his wife, and they will become one flesh. The man and his wife were both <u>naked</u>, and they felt no <u>shame</u>.

Now the <u>serpent</u> was more crafty than any of the wild animals the LORD God had made ... When the woman <u>saw</u> that the fruit of the tree was good for food and pleasing to the eye, and also <u>desirable</u> for gaining wisdom, she took some and ate it. She also gave some to her <u>husband</u>, who was with her, and he ate it. Then the eyes of both of them were opened, and they <u>realized</u> they were naked; so they <u>sewed</u> <u>fig</u> <u>leaves</u> together and made <u>coverings</u> for themselves.

To the woman he said, "I will <u>greatly</u> increase your pains in <u>childbearing</u>; with <u>pain</u> you will give birth to children. Your desire will be for your husband, and he will rule over you." To Adam he said, "Because you listened to your <u>wife</u> and <u>ate</u> from the tree about which I commanded you, 'You must not eat of it,' "<u>Cursed</u> is the ground because of you; through painful toil you will eat of it all the days of your life.

Adam named his wife Eve, because she would become the <u>mother</u> of all the living.

Adam lay with his wife Eve, and she became <u>pregnant</u> and gave birth to Cain. She said, "With the help of the LORD I have brought forth a man." <u>Later</u> she gave birth to his brother Abel. (Genesis 1:27-28; 2:18, 21-25; 3:1, 6-7, 16-17, 20; 4:1-2 NIV)

Bible Word Search, Vol. II: Women in the Bible

```
Y H E N E L B A T I U S E R G
D L S L A W I F E P B G E N D
E R T E A K D Y L V A P I E P
S E G A L M E A T M L R S E E
I A P S E F E D I E A R E A C
R L U Z H R S F H E U L K T D
A I N B I R G G B C S M S E N
B Z I K F S M D N S E L R B A
L E A N E O L H S I E M H D M
E D P W T I U D T E R V A D O
A Q E H H S L A T A R E A H W
Q D E C B F I G Z I K P V E S
W R I A B K K E N O B E E O L
A S N J T N A N G E R P N N C
S D Z G V N L U F T I U R F T
```

COPYRIGHT © GIL PUBLICATIONS 2006

10. Eve

ATE	GREATLY	RIB
BONE	HELPER	SAW
CHILDBEARING	HUSBAND	SERPENT
COVERINGS	IMAGE	SEWED
CURSED	LEAVES	SHAME
DESIRABLE	MOTHER	SLEEP
FEMALE	NAKED	SUITABLE
FIG	PAIN	TAKEN
FLESH	PREGNANT	WIFE
FRUITFUL	REALIZED	WOMAN

GIL Publications, P. O. Box 80275, Brooklyn, NY 11208
www.BibleWordSearchPuzzles.com

11. Great Woman of Shunem

And it fell on a day, that <u>Elisha</u> passed to <u>Shunem</u>, where *was* a <u>great</u> woman; and she <u>constrained</u> him to eat bread. And *so* it was, *that* as oft as he passed by, he turned in <u>thither</u> to eat bread. And she said unto her husband, <u>Behold</u> now, I <u>perceive</u> that this *is* an holy man of God, which <u>passeth</u> by us continually. Let us make a little <u>chamber</u>, I pray thee, on the wall; and let us set for him there a <u>bed</u>, and a <u>table</u>, and a <u>stool</u>, and a <u>candlestick</u>: and it shall be, when he cometh to us, that he shall turn in thither.

And it fell on a day, that he came thither, and he turned into the chamber, and lay there. And he said to <u>Gehazi</u> his servant, Call this <u>Shunammite</u>. And when he had called her, she stood before him.

And he said, What then *is* to be done for her? And Gehazi answered, Verily she hath no <u>child</u>, and her husband is old. And he said, Call her. And when he had called her, she stood in the <u>door</u>. And he said, About this season, according to the time of life, thou shalt <u>embrace</u> a son. And she said, Nay, my lord, *thou* man of God, do not lie unto thine <u>handmaid</u>. And the woman <u>conceived</u>, and bare a son at that <u>season</u> that Elisha had said unto her, according to the time of life.

And when the child was <u>grown</u>, it fell on a day, that he went out to his father to the <u>reapers</u>. And he said unto his father, My <u>head</u>, my head. And he said to a lad, Carry him to his mother. And when he had taken him, and brought him to his mother, he sat on her <u>knees</u> till noon, and *then* died. And she went up, and <u>laid</u> him on the bed of the man of God, and shut *the door* upon him, and went out.

And when Elisha was come into the house, behold, the child was dead, *and* laid upon his bed.

Then he returned, and <u>walked</u> in the house to and fro; and went up, and <u>stretched</u> himself upon him: and the child <u>sneezed</u> seven times, and the child opened his eyes.

Then she went in, and fell at his feet, and bowed herself to the <u>ground</u>, and took up her son, and went out.

(2 Kings 4: 8-12, 14-21, 32, 35, 37 KJV)

Bible Word Search, Vol. II: Women in the Bible

11. Great Woman of Shunem

BED	GEHAZI	REAPERS
BEHOLD	GREAT	SEASON
CANDLESTICK	GROUND	SHUNEM
CHAMBER	GROWN	SHUNAMMITE
CHILD	HANDMAID	SNEEZED
CONCEIVED	HEAD	STOOL
CONSTRAINED	KNEES	STRETCHED
DOOR	LAID	TABLE
ELISHA	PASSETH	THITHER
EMBRACE	PERCEIVE	WALKED

GIL Publications, P. O. Box 80275, Brooklyn, NY 11208
www.BibleWordSearchPuzzles.com

12. Hagar

Now Sarai, Abram's wife, had borne him no children. But she had an Egyptian maidservant named Hagar; so she said to Abram, "The LORD has kept me from having children. Go, sleep with my maidservant; perhaps I can build a family through her." ...after Abram had been living in Canaan ten years, Sarai his wife took her Egyptian maidservant Hagar and gave her to her husband to be his wife. He slept with Hagar, and she conceived.

When she knew she was pregnant, she began to despise her mistress. Then Sarai said to Abram, "You are responsible for the wrong I am suffering. I put my servant in your arms, and now that she knows she is pregnant, she despises me. May the LORD judge between you and me."

"Your servant is in your hands," Abram said. "Do with her whatever you think best." Then Sarai mistreated Hagar; so she fled from her.

The angel of the LORD found Hagar near a spring in the desert; it was the spring that is beside the road to Shur. And he said, "Hagar, servant of Sarai, where have you come from, and where are you going?"

"I'm running away from my mistress Sarai," she answered.

Then the angel of the LORD told her, "Go back to your mistress and submit to her." The angel added, "I will so increase your descendants that they will be too numerous to count."

"You are now with child and you will have a son. You shall name him Ishmael, for the LORD has heard of your misery. He will be a wild donkey of a man; his hand will be against everyone and everyone's hand against him, and he will live in hostility toward all his brothers."

She gave this name to the LORD who spoke to her: "You are the God who sees me," for she said, "I have now seen the One who sees me." That is why the well was called Beer Lahai Roi; it is still there, between Kadesh and Bered. (Genesis 16:1-11 NIV)

For it is written that Abraham had two sons, one by the slave woman and the other by the free woman. His son by the slave woman was born in the ordinary way; but his son by the free woman was born as the result of a promise.

These things may be taken figuratively, for the women represent two covenants. One covenant is from Mount Sinai and bears children who are to be slaves: This is Hagar. Now Hagar stands for Mount Sinai in Arabia and corresponds to the present city of Jerusalem, because she is in slavery with her children. But the Jerusalem that is above is free, and she is our mother. (Galatians 4:22-26 NIV)

Bible Word Search, Vol. II: Women in the Bible

```
S F M J M C D L I W I H E R B
S C O U N T O T Y L R O A D G
F A M I L Y K V L E H U S D E
A N A B R A M W E A K Y F E M
U A I U R L I R E N I N O L T
L A D L I H C I E S A B O F S
E N S U B M I T K S I N A D E
A E E R F T S T W A I P T R B
M B R A G A H E H K D M S V A
H Y V Z I S U N X J F E O E M
S L A V E J R G G D A Q S R D
I D N M L U V Q S O N O T H P
R C T N Z D F A R M S B C G S
S P R I N G N P Q J I A R A S
R Y M N Y E A N A I T P Y G E
```

COPYRIGHT © GIL PUBLICATIONS 2006

12. Hagar

ABRAM	EGYPTIAN	PROMISE
ARABIA	FAMILY	ROAD
ARMS	FLED	SARAI
BEST	FREE	SHUR
CANAAN	HAGAR	SLAVE
CHILD	HER	SON
COUNT	ISHMAEL	SPRING
COVENANT	JUDGE	SUBMIT
DESPISE	KADESH	WILD
DONKEY	MAIDSERVANT	WRITTEN

GIL Publications, P. O. Box 80275, Brooklyn, NY 11208
www.BibleWordSearchPuzzles.com

13. Hannah

Now there was a certain man of Ramathaimzophim …his name *was* Elkanah … he had two wives … Peninnah had children, but Hannah had no children. And this man went up out of his city yearly to worship and to sacrifice unto the LORD of hosts in Shiloh … when the time was that Elkanah offered, he gave to Peninnah his wife, and to all her sons and her daughters, portions: But unto Hannah he gave a worthy portion; for he loved Hannah: but the LORD had shut up her womb. And her adversary also provoked her sore, for to make her fret, because the LORD had shut up her womb… therefore she wept, and did not eat. Then said Elkanah her husband to her, Hannah, why weepest thou? and why eatest thou not? and why is thy heart grieved? *am* not I better to thee than ten sons?

So Hannah rose up after they had eaten in Shiloh, and … drunk. Now Eli the priest sat upon a seat by a post of the temple of the LORD. And she *was* in bitterness of soul, and prayed unto the LORD, and wept sore. And she vowed a vow … O LORD of hosts, if thou wilt indeed look on the affliction of thine handmaid, and remember me, and not forget thine handmaid, but wilt give unto thine handmaid a man child, then I will give him unto the LORD all the days of his life, and there shall no razor come upon his head. And it came to pass, as she continued praying before the LORD, that Eli marked her mouth.

And they rose up in the morning early, and worshipped before the LORD, and returned, and came to their house to Ramah: and Elkanah knew Hannah his wife; and the LORD remembered her. Wherefore it came to pass, when the time was come about after Hannah had conceived, that she bare a son, and called his name Samuel, *saying*, Because I have asked him of the LORD …

And when she had weaned him, she took him up with her, with three bullocks, and one ephah of flour, and a bottle of wine, and brought him unto the house of the LORD in Shiloh: and the child *was* young. And they slew a bullock, and brought the child to Eli. And she said, Oh my lord, *as* thy soul liveth, my lord, I *am* the woman that stood by thee here, praying unto the LORD. For this child I prayed; and the LORD hath given me my petition which I asked of him: Therefore also I have lent him to the LORD; as long as he liveth he shall be lent to the LORD. And he worshipped the LORD there. (1 Samuel 1:1-12, 19-20, 24-24 KJV)

And Hannah prayed, and said, My heart rejoiceth in the LORD, mine horn is exalted in the LORD: my mouth is enlarged over mine enemies; because I rejoice in thy salvation. *There is* none holy as the LORD: for *there is* none beside thee: neither *is there* any rock like our God.

And the LORD visited Hannah … she conceived, and bare three sons and two daughters … Samuel grew before the LORD. (1 Samuel 2:1-2, 21 KJV)

Bible Word Search, Vol. II: Women in the Bible

```
H X T E M P L E H A N A K L E
A D V E R S A R Y L R A E Y N
N E B Z C W E N O I T R O P L
D X N E E N X H A N N A H Y A
M M K A R B L X S F P I H Z R
A I N P V U I Q I O U O G Q G
I E U X N W I D D A Z Q J A E
D H R P L M F L E X A L T E D
S A D I E A H E A D E Y A R P
H N E H U K E C I F I R C A S
I N R S M Q M Q R U Y W O M B
L I E R A E T O L O V E D A S
O N F O S N Z E Q I C E I H O
H E F W E A N N M R Q K U L R
I P O W R T J A H O S T S K E
```

COPYRIGHT © GIL PUBLICATIONS 2006

13. Hannah

ADVERSARY	LENT	SAMUEL
DRUNK	LOVED	SHILOH
ELI	OFFERED	SHUT
ELKANAH	PENINNAH	SORE
ENLARGED	PORTION	TEMPLE
EXALTED	PRAYED	WEANED
HANDMAID	RAMAH	WENT
HANNAH	RAZOR	WOMB
HEAD	ROCK	WORSHIP
HOSTS	SACRIFICE	YEARLY

GIL Publications, P. O. Box 80275, Brooklyn, NY 11208
www.BibleWordSearchPuzzles.com

14. Jael

Sisera, however, fled on foot to the tent of <u>Jael</u>, the wife of <u>Heber</u> the <u>Kenite</u>, because there were friendly <u>relations</u> between <u>Jabin</u> king of <u>Hazor</u> and the <u>clan</u> of Heber the Kenite.
Jael went out to meet Sisera and said to him, "Come, my lord, come right in. Don't be afraid." So he <u>entered</u> her tent, and she put a <u>covering</u> over him.
"I'm thirsty," he said. "Please give me some <u>water</u>." She opened a <u>skin</u> of <u>milk</u>, gave him a <u>drink</u>, and covered him up.
"Stand in the <u>doorway</u> of the tent," he <u>told</u> her. "If someone comes by and asks you, 'Is anyone here?' say 'No.'"
But Jael, Heber's wife, <u>picked</u> up a tent <u>peg</u> and a hammer and went quietly to him while he lay fast asleep, <u>exhausted</u>. She drove the peg through his temple into the <u>ground</u>, and he died.
<u>Barak</u> came by in <u>pursuit</u> of Sisera, and Jael went out to meet him. "Come," she said, "I will show you the man you're looking for." So he went in with her, and there lay Sisera with the tent peg through his temple—dead.

"Most <u>blessed</u> of women be Jael,
    the wife of Heber the Kenite,
    most blessed of tent-<u>dwelling</u> women.
He asked for water, and she gave him milk;
    in a bowl <u>fit</u> for <u>nobles</u> she brought him <u>curdled</u> milk.
Her hand reached for the tent peg,
    her right hand for the <u>workman's</u> hammer.
She struck Sisera, she <u>crushed</u> his head,
    she <u>shattered</u> and pierced his temple.
At her feet he sank,
    he fell; there he lay.
At her feet he <u>sank</u>, he fell;
    where he sank, there he fell—dead.
        (Judges 4:17-22; 5:24-27 NIV)

Bible Word Search, Vol. II: Women in the Bible

```
J A E L D O O R W A Y S A N K
A R O Z A H E B E R S K I N E
B E N T E R E D N U O R G O N
I T T W O R K M A N S S E B I
N A I R A J D N M Q V N P L T
A W F F E A B U D R K O I E E
L C D D U D F T E J P I C S X
C O E D P R T L U R I T K P H
U V H E F O M T G G X A E U A
R E S I S C M V J H P L D R U
D R U Y R G T M Z D F E L S S
L I R T H H X R R C Z R O U T
E N C D E R E T T A H S T I E
D G N I L L E W D K L I M T D
D E S S E L B A R A K N I R D
```

Copyright © Gil Publications 2006

14. Jael

BARAK	EXHAUSTED	PEG
BLESSED	FIT	PICKED
CLAN	GROUND	PURSUIT
COVERING	HAZOR	RELATIONS
CRUSHED	HEBER	SANK
CURDLED	JABIN	SHATTERED
DOORWAY	JAEL	SKIN
DRINK	KENITE	TOLD
DWELLING	MILK	WATER
ENTERED	NOBLES	WORKMANS

15. Jephthah's Daughter

And Jephthah vowed a vow unto the LORD, and said, If thou shalt without fail deliver the children of Ammon into mine hands, Then it shall be, that whatsoever cometh forth of the doors of my house to meet me, when I return in peace from the children of Ammon, shall surely be the LORD'S, and I will offer it up for a burnt offering. So Jephthah passed over unto the children of Ammon to fight against them; and the LORD delivered them into his hands. And he smote them from Aroer, even till thou come to Minnith, *even* twenty cities, and unto the plain of the vineyards, with a very great slaughter. Thus the children of Ammon were subdued before the children of Israel. And Jephthah came to Mizpeh unto his house, and, behold, his daughter came out to meet him with timbrels and with dances: and she *was his* only child; beside her he had neither son nor daughter. And it came to pass, when he saw her, that he rent his clothes, and said, Alas, my daughter! thou hast brought me very low, and thou art one of them that trouble me: for I have opened my mouth unto the LORD, and I cannot go back. And she said unto him, My father, *if* thou hast opened thy mouth unto the LORD, do to me according to that which hath proceeded out of thy mouth; forasmuch as the LORD hath taken vengeance for thee of thine enemies, *even* of the children of Ammon. And she said unto her father, Let this thing be done for me: let me alone two months, that I may go up and down upon the mountains, and bewail my virginity, I and my fellows. And he said, Go. And he sent her away *for* two months: and she went with her companions, and bewailed her virginity upon the mountains. And it came to pass at the end of two months, that she returned unto her father, who did with her *according* to his vow which he had vowed: and she knew no man. And it was a custom in Israel, *That* the daughters of Israel went yearly to lament the daughter of Jephthah the Gileadite four days in a year. (Judges 11:30-40 KJV)

Bible Word Search, Vol. II: Women in the Bible

```
D A N C E S X V Y K U P L Q P
T S A L A M E N T Z S F U X C
K U M I R O B Q N W O D Z O R
F B M A O T K E E M U N J F F
O D O F E E N S W O L L E F G
R U N P R N E A T A L G Q E S
A E M E D E W O V A I K C R N
S D R A Y E N I V N W L H I O
M U Y C G I L E A D I T E N I
U S L E R B M I T C U S H G N
C E N E M I E S V O V A A Y A
H B Y R Z Z E G M E A H N Z P
L Y A P R E L B U O R T D R M
P N E R D L I H C T Z Y S L O
R H T I N N I M A P K S F D C
```

COPYRIGHT © GIL PUBLICATIONS 2006

15. Title

- ALAS
- AMMON
- AROER
- BEWAIL
- CHILDREN
- COMPANIONS
- DANCES
- DELIVER
- DOWN
- ENEMIES
- FAIL
- FELLOWS
- FORASMUCH
- GILEADITE
- HANDS
- HAST
- KNEW
- LAMENT
- MINNITH
- MIZPEH
- MOUTH
- OFFERING
- PEACE
- SMOTE
- SUBDUED
- TIMBRELS
- TROUBLE
- TWENTY
- VINEYARDS
- VOWED

16. Jezebel

Ahab son of Omri did more evil in the eyes of the LORD than any of those before him. He not only considered it trivial to commit the sins of Jeroboam son of Nebat, but he also married Jezebel daughter of Ethbaal king of the Sidonians, and began to serve Baal and worship him. (1 Kings 16:30-31 NLT)

Meanwhile, the famine had become very severe in Samaria. So Ahab summoned Obadiah, who was in charge of the palace. (Now Obadiah was a devoted follower of the LORD. Once when Jezebel had tried to kill all the LORD'S prophets, Obadiah had hidden one hundred of them in two caves. He had put fifty prophets in each cave and had supplied them with food and water. (1 Kings 18:2-4 NLT)

Now Ahab told Jezebel everything Elijah had done and how he had killed all the prophets with the sword. So Jezebel sent a messenger to Elijah to say, "May the gods deal with me, be it ever so severely, if by this time tomorrow I do not make your life like that of one of them." Elijah was afraid and ran for his life. (1 Kings 19:1-3 NIV)

… after these things … Naboth the Jezreelite had a vineyard, which *was* in Jezreel, hard by the palace of Ahab … Ahab spake unto Naboth, saying, Give me thy vineyard, that I may have it for a garden of herbs, … Naboth said to Ahab, The LORD forbid it me, that I should give the inheritance of my fathers unto thee. And Ahab came into his house heavy and displeased … But Jezebel his wife came to him, and said unto him, Why is thy spirit so sad, that thou eatest no bread … Dost thou now govern the kingdom of Israel? … I will give thee the vineyard … she wrote letters in Ahab's name … unto the elders and to the nobles … saying, Proclaim a fast, and set Naboth on high among the people: And set two men, sons of Belial, before him, to bear witness against him, saying, Thou didst blaspheme God and the king. And *then* carry him out, and stone him, that he may die … And the men of his city … did as Jezebel had sent unto them (1 Kings 21:1-11 KJV)

"This is what the LORD, the God of Israel, says … I will avenge the murder of my prophets and all the LORD'S servants who were killed by Jezebel. The entire family of Ahab must be wiped out … Dogs will eat Ahab's wife, Jezebel, at the plot of land in Jezreel, and no one will bury her. (2 Kings 9:6-10 NLT)

Bible Word Search, Vol. II: Women in the Bible

```
R T W S A H A B E E S M V C B
L E P N S E V A C L I B U R Y
X P H T A R B A A A C V E E H
D I L F B B J L L I K A X G R
K H D O G S O C A C D Y D N K
N S E B T A O T P S T O N E P
O R X A C R R P H D P S N S M
B O G D P Y C D I L P H E S U
L W X I V W W B E X E L E E R
E C N A T I R E H N I R L M D
S T E H P O R P I J P B O Y E
I H R E F Z U M A O B T W Q R
F K D L E V A H O J B G L T B
U N N J W F S C N U U F M R R
K E O Q E P K J E Z E B E L Z
```

COPYRIGHT © GIL PUBLICATIONS 2006

16. Jezebel

AHAB	GARDEN	NOBLES
BAAL	HEAVY	OBADIAH
BLASPHEME	HERBS	OMRI
BREAD	INHERITANCE	PALACE
BURY	JEZEBEL	PLOT
CAVES	JEZREEL	PROCLAIM
DOGS	KILL	PROPHETS
ELIJAH	MESSENGER	STONE
FAMINE	MURDER	WIPED
FORBID	NABOTH	WORSHIP

GIL Publications, P. O. Box 80275, Brooklyn, NY 11208
www.BibleWordSearchPuzzles.com

17. Jochebed, Moses' Mother

And the name of Amram's wife *was* <u>Jochebed</u>, the daughter of Levi, whom *her mother* bare to Levi in Egypt: and she bare unto <u>Amram</u> Aaron and Moses, and Miriam their sister. (Numbers 26:59 KJV)

And there went a man of the house of <u>Levi</u>, and took *to wife* a daughter of Levi. And the woman conceived, and <u>bare</u> a son: and when she saw him that he was a <u>goodly</u> <u>child</u>, she hid him three months. And when she could not longer hide him, she took for him an <u>ark</u> of <u>bulrushes</u>, and <u>daubed</u> it with <u>slime</u> and with <u>pitch</u>, and put the child therein; and she <u>laid</u> it in the <u>flags</u> by the river's brink. And his sister stood <u>afar</u> off, to <u>wit</u> what would be done to him.

And the daughter of <u>Pharaoh</u> came down to wash *herself* at the <u>river</u>; and her <u>maidens</u> walked along by the river's <u>side</u>; and when she saw the ark among the flags, she sent her maid to <u>fetch</u> it. And when she had <u>opened</u> *it*, she saw the child: and, behold, the <u>babe</u> wept. And she had <u>compassion</u> on him, and said, This *is one* of the Hebrews' children. Then said his sister to Pharaoh's daughter, Shall I go and call to thee a <u>nurse</u> of the <u>Hebrew</u> women, that she may nurse the child for thee? And Pharaoh's daughter said to her, Go. And the maid went and called the child's <u>mother</u>. And Pharaoh's daughter said unto her, Take this child away, and nurse it for me, and I will give *thee* thy <u>wages</u>. And the woman took the child, and nursed it. And the child grew, and she brought him unto Pharaoh's daughter, and he became her son. And she called his name <u>Moses</u>: and she said, Because I <u>drew</u> him out of the <u>water</u>.
(Exodus 2:1-20 KJV)

Bible Word Search, Vol. II: Women in the Bible

```
W L E J D M B U L R U S H E S
E E S R U N O I S S A P M O C
G K A B H Q P D E B E H C O J
T N J E H C T I P H A R A O H
A R B C S W B B S N E D I A M
A I S U Z M A R M A D Y O W M
R V U X J F B R A F A L P E O
K E E W A K I N Z Y U D E R T
V R N T K T G E R A B O N B H
B K A D V R Y B A B E O E E E
C W I K K T I W E R D G D H R
D D N W I V E L A I D L I H C
O E G S K S S G A L F E T C H
K X M G J S P E D I S L I M E
F Z R E T A W A G E S E S O M
```

COPYRIGHT © GIL PUBLICATIONS 2006

17. Jochebed, Moses' Mother

AFAR	FETCH	NURSE
AMRAM	FLAGS	OPENED
ARK	GOODLY	PHARAOH
BABE	HEBREW	PITCH
BARE	JOCHEBED	RIVER
BULRUSHES	LAID	SIDE
CHILD	LEVI	SLIME
COMPASSION	MAIDENS	WAGES
DAUBED	MOSES	WATER
DREW	MOTHER	WIT

GIL Publications, P. O. Box 80275, Brooklyn, NY 11208
www.BibleWordSearchPuzzles.com

18. Leah

And Laban had two daughters ... the elder *was* Leah, and ... younger *was* Rachel. Leah *was* tender eyed; but Rachel was beautiful and well favoured. And Jacob loved Rachel; and said, I will serve thee seven years for Rachel thy younger daughter ...

And Jacob served seven years for Rachel; and they seemed unto him *but* a few days, for the love he had to her...And it came to pass in the evening, that he took Leah his daughter, and brought her to him; and he went in unto her ... And it came to pass, that in the morning, behold, it *was* Leah: and he said to Laban, What *is* this thou hast done unto me? did not I serve with thee for Rachel? wherefore then hast thou beguiled me?

And he went in also unto Rachel, and he loved also Rachel more than Leah, and served with him yet seven other years. And when the LORD saw that Leah *was* hated, he opened her womb: but Rachel *was* barren ...

And Leah conceived, and bare a son, and she called his name Reuben: for she said, Surely the LORD hath looked upon my affliction; now therefore my husband will love me...

And she conceived again ... Simeon ... Levi ... Judah ...

And Leah said, A troop cometh: ... Gad. And Zilpah Leah's maid bare Jacob a second son. And Leah said, Happy am I, for the daughters will call me blessed: and she called his name Asher.

And she said unto her [Rachel], *Is it* a small matter that thou hast taken my husband? and wouldest thou take away my son's mandrakes also? And Rachel said, Therefore he shall lie with thee to night for thy son's mandrakes ...

... Issachar ... Then she [Leah] became pregnant again and had a sixth son. She named him Zebulun, for she said, "God has given me good gifts for my husband. Now he will honor me, for I have given him six sons." Later she gave birth to a daughter and named her Dinah....

(Genesis 29:16-18, 20, 23, 25, 30-31, 32, 33, 34, 35; 30: 11-13, 15, 18, 20-21 KJV)

Bible Word Search, Vol. II: Women in the Bible

```
D Q S E H A D U J F G L R P Y
N A B A L E H C A R P E E R D
M D T E N D E R C O S V S E E
V W A H S V E M O R N I N G T
P H T H G U O R B R M E J N A
O E M U O N T H E E D I N A H
Z R S G R N E K O U R S O N S
N E A E I D O N K B Y S I T R
U F B A K S E R V E V A T K E
L O J V X A T I Z N V C C Q T
U R A S H E R R T D X H I Q H
B E G U I L E D A U O A L K G
E Z U Z D X W A N T D R F T U
Z I L P A H T G R A G E F F A
I X C O M E T H O G M D A O D
```

COPYRIGHT © GIL PUBLICATIONS 2006

18. Leah

AFFLICTION	HONOR	RACHEL
ASHER	ISSACHAR	REUBEN
BEGUILED	JACOB	SERVE
BROUGHT	JUDAH	SIMEON
COMETH	LABAN	SIXTH
DAUGHTERS	LEAH	TENDER
DINAH	LEVI	TROOP
ELDER	MANDRAKES	WHEREFORE
GAD	MORNING	ZEBULUN
HATED	PREGNANT	ZILPAH

GIL Publications, P. O. Box 80275, Brooklyn, NY 11208
www.BibleWordSearchPuzzles.com

19. Lot's Wife and Two Daughters

At dawn the next morning the angels became insistent. "Hurry," they said to <u>Lot</u>. "Take your wife and your two <u>daughters</u> who are here. Get out of here right now, or you will be caught in the destruction of the city."

When Lot still <u>hesitated</u>, the angels <u>seized</u> his hand and the hands of his wife and two daughters and rushed them to safety outside the city, for the LORD was <u>merciful</u>. "Run for your lives!" the angels <u>warned</u>. "Do not stop anywhere in the valley. And don't look back! <u>Escape</u> to the mountains, or you will die."

"Oh no, my lords, please," Lot begged ... I cannot go to the mountains. Disaster would catch up to me there, and I would soon die. See, there is a small village nearby. Please let me go there instead; don't you see how small it is? Then my life will be saved."

"All right," the angel said, "I will grant your request. I will not destroy that little village. But <u>hurry</u>! For I can do nothing until you are there." From that time on, that village was known as <u>Zoar</u>.

The <u>sun</u> was rising as Lot reached the village. Then the LORD rained down fire and burning <u>sulfur</u> from the heavens on <u>Sodom</u> and <u>Gomorrah</u>. He utterly destroyed them, along with the other cities and villages of the plain, eliminating all life--people, <u>plants</u>, and <u>animals</u> alike. But Lot's <u>wife</u> <u>looked</u> back as she was following along behind him, and she became a <u>pillar</u> of <u>salt</u>. (Genesis 19:12-27 NLT)

Afterward Lot left Zoar because he was <u>afraid</u> of the people there, and he went to live in a cave in the mountains with his two daughters. One day the older daughter said to her sister, "There isn't a man anywhere in this entire area for us to <u>marry</u>. And our father will soon be too old to have <u>children</u>. Come, let's get him <u>drunk</u> with <u>wine</u>, and then we will sleep with him. That way we will preserve our family line through our father." So that night they got him drunk, and the older daughter went in and slept with her father ...the younger daughter went in and slept with him. As before, he was <u>unaware</u> of her lying down or getting up again. So both of Lot's daughters became <u>pregnant</u> by their father.

When the older daughter gave birth to a son, she named him Moab. He became the ancestor of the nation now known as the <u>Moabites</u>. When the <u>younger</u> daughter gave birth to a son, she named him Ben-ammi. He became the <u>ancestor</u> of the nation now known as the <u>Ammonites</u>. (Genesis 19:30-37 NLT)

Bible Word Search, Vol. II: Women in the Bible

19. Lot's Wife and Two Daughters

AFRAID	HURRY	SEIZED
AMMONITES	LOOKED	SODOM
ANCESTOR	LOT	SULFUR
ANIMALS	MARRY	SUN
CHILDREN	MERCIFUL	UNAWARE
DAUGHTERS	MOABITES	WARNED
DRUNK	PILLAR	WIFE
ESCAPE	PLANTS	WINE
GOMORRAH	PREGNANT	YOUNGER
HESITATED	SALT	ZOAR

GIL Publications, P. O. Box 80275, Brooklyn, NY 11208
www.BibleWordSearchPuzzles.com

20. Maid of Naaman's Wife

Now <u>Naaman</u>, <u>captain</u> of the host of the king of Syria, was a great man with his master, and <u>honourable</u>, because by him the LORD had given deliverance unto Syria: he was also a <u>mighty</u> man in <u>valour</u>, *but he was* a <u>leper</u>. [2]And the Syrians had gone out by companies, and had brought away <u>captive</u> out of the land of Israel a little <u>maid</u>; and she waited on Naaman's wife. [3]And she said unto her <u>mistress</u>, Would God my lord *were* with the <u>prophet</u> that *is* in <u>Samaria</u>! for he would <u>recover</u> him of his leprosy. [4]And one went in, and told his lord, saying, Thus and thus said the maid that *is* of the land of Israel.

And the king of <u>Syria</u> said, Go to, go, and I will send a letter unto the king of Israel. And he <u>departed</u>, and took with him ten <u>talents</u> of silver, and six <u>thousand</u> *pieces* of gold, and ten changes of <u>raiment</u>. [6]And he brought the letter to the king of Israel, saying, Now when this letter is come unto thee, behold, I have *therewith* sent Naaman my servant to thee, that thou <u>mayest</u> recover him of his leprosy. [7]And it came to pass, when the king of Israel had read the <u>letter</u>, that he rent his clothes, and said, *Am* I God, to kill and to make alive, that this man doth send unto me to recover a man of his leprosy? wherefore <u>consider</u>, I pray you, and see how he seeketh a <u>quarrel</u> against me.

And it was *so*, when Elisha the man of God had heard that the king of Israel had <u>rent</u> his clothes, that he sent to the king, saying, Wherefore hast thou rent thy clothes? let him come now to me, and he shall know that there is a prophet in Israel.

[9]So Naaman came with his <u>horses</u> and with his <u>chariot</u>, and stood at the door of the house of Elisha.

Then went he down, and <u>dipped</u> himself seven times in <u>Jordan</u>, according to the saying of the man of God: and his flesh came again like unto the flesh of a <u>little</u> child, and he was <u>clean</u>.

[15]And he returned to the man of God, he and all his <u>company</u>, and came, and stood <u>before</u> him: and he said, Behold, now I know that *there is* no God in all the earth, but in Israel: now therefore, I pray thee, take a blessing of thy servant. (2 Kings 5: 1-9, 14-15 KJV)

Bible Word Search, Vol. II: Women in the Bible

```
A I R A M A S S E R T S I M
R E D I S N O C T E H P O R P
E L T T I L R E V O C E R H X
T J V P X E T N E M A I R O T
T H O U S A N D N A M A A N G
E O Z Q C I E K Q N A D R O J
L O D L Z T R S E U M J X U U
C S E S R O H V V A L O U R L
Y A P A V Q T O I R A H C A Q
N V P M A Y E S T M S A U B C
L E I T T C O M P A N Y P L R
D B D H A X B J A E R O F E B
I H G P U I X K C B K W P M Z
A I R Y S D N S S T N E L A T
M U K K Q U A R R E L G F Z M
```

COPYRIGHT © GIL PUBLICATIONS 2006

20. Maid of Naaman's Wife

BEFORE	HORSES	PROPHET
CAPTAIN	JORDAN	QUARREL
CAPTIVE	LEPER	RECOVER
CHARIOT	LETTER	RENT
CLEAN	LITTLE	RIAMENT
COMPANY	MAID	SAMARIA
CONSIDER	MAYEST	SYRIA
DEPARTED	MIGHTY	TALENTS
DIPPED	MISTRESS	THOUSAND
HONOURABLE	NAAMAN	VALOUR

GIL Publications, P. O. Box 80275, Brooklyn, NY 11208
www.BibleWordSearchPuzzles.com

21. Michal

Now the sons of <u>Saul</u> were <u>Jonathan</u>, and <u>Ishui</u>, and <u>Melchishua</u>: and the names of his two daughters *were these*; the name of the firstborn <u>Merab</u>, and the name of the younger <u>Michal</u>...
But it came to pass at the time when Merab Saul's daughter should have been given to David, that she was given unto <u>Adriel</u> the <u>Meholathite</u> to wife. And Michal Saul's daughter loved David: and they told Saul, and the thing pleased him. And Saul said, I will give him her, that she may be a <u>snare</u> to him, and that the hand of the Philistines may be against him. Wherefore Saul said to David, Thou shalt this day be my son in law in *the one of* the <u>twain</u>.

And Saul said, Thus shall ye say to David, The king desireth not any <u>dowry</u>, but an hundred <u>foreskins</u> of the Philistines, to be <u>avenged</u> of the king's enemies. But Saul thought to make David fall by the hand of the Philistines. And when his servants told David these words, it pleased David well to be the king's son in law: and the days were not <u>expired</u>. Wherefore David arose and went, he and his men, and slew of the Philistines two hundred men ... Saul gave him Michal ... Saul saw and knew that the LORD *was* with David, and *that* Michal ... loved him. And Saul was yet the more afraid of David; and Saul became David's enemy continually.

Saul also sent messengers unto David's house, to watch him, and to slay him in the morning: and Michal David's wife told him, saying, If thou save not thy life to night, to morrow thou shalt be slain. So Michal let David down through a window: and he went, and <u>fled</u>, and <u>escaped</u>. And Michal took an <u>image</u>, and laid *it* in the bed, and put a pillow of goats' *hair* for his <u>bolster</u>, and covered *it* with a cloth... And Saul said unto Michal, Why hast thou deceived me so, and sent away mine enemy ...

And <u>Abigail</u> hasted, and arose, and rode upon an ass, with five damsels of hers that went after her; and she went after the messengers of David, and became his wife. David also took <u>Ahinoam</u> of <u>Jezreel</u>; and they were also both of them his wives. But Saul had given Michal his daughter, David's wife, to <u>Phalti</u> the son of <u>Laish</u>, which *was* of <u>Gallim</u>. (1 Samuel 14:49; 18:19-21, 25-29; 19:11-13, 17; 25:42-44 KJV)

And David sent messengers to <u>Ishbosheth</u> Saul's son, saying, Deliver *me* my wife Michal, which I <u>espoused</u> to me for an hundred foreskins ...

So David and all the house of Israel brought up the ark of the LORD with shouting, and with the sound of the trumpet. And as the ark of the LORD came into the city of David, Michal Saul's daughter looked through a <u>window</u>, and saw king David <u>leaping</u> and <u>dancing</u> before the LORD; and she <u>despised</u> him in her heart ...Therefore Michal the daughter of Saul had no child unto the day of her death. (2 Samuel 3:14; 6:15-16, 23 KJV)

Bible Word Search, Vol. II: Women in the Bible

```
A A U H S I H C L E M L V J L
V H T E H S O B H S I I T Y E
E T I H T A L O H E M T T T A
N Q V N L E I H S I A L E P P
G E H T O G E C M O U A M A I
E M I L L A G D E N A H F D N
D L S Y L M M E R T N P S R G
E E D N W I P R A L A H C I M
S E E L I A G I B A H F L E D
P R S E N K V P G I T U S L A
I Z U S D D S X S Y A W N H N
S E O D O P H E S S N G A E C
E J P R W W J Y R W O D R I I
D S X E S C A P E O J T E H N
Z R E T S L O B Q V F L T X G
```

COPYRIGHT © GIL PUBLICATIONS 2006

21. Michal

- ABIGAIL
- ADRIEL
- AHINOAM
- AVENGED
- BOLSTER
- DANCING
- DESPISED
- DOWRY
- ESCAPE
- EXPIRED
- EXPOUSED
- FLED
- FORESKINS
- GALLIM
- IMAGE
- ISHBOSHETH
- ISHUI
- JEZREEL
- JONATHAN
- LAISH
- LEAPING
- MEHOLATHITE
- MELCHISHUA
- MERAB
- MICHAL
- PHALTI
- SAUL
- SNARE
- TWAIN
- WINDOW

GIL Publications, P. O. Box 80275, Brooklyn, NY 11208
www.BibleWordSearchPuzzles.com

22. Miriam

... <u>Amram</u>'s wife was named <u>Jochebed</u> ... a descendant of <u>Levi</u> ... in the land of Egypt. Amram and Jochebed became the <u>parents</u> of <u>Aaron</u>, <u>Moses</u>, and their sister, <u>Miriam</u>. (Numbers 26:59 NLT)

... when she [Moses' mother] could hide him no longer, she ... placed the child in it [basket] and put it among the reeds along the bank of the Nile. His sister stood at a distance to see what would happen to him ... Pharaoh's daughter went down to the <u>Nile</u> to bathe ... She saw the basket among the reeds and sent her slave girl to get it ... Then his <u>sister</u> asked Pharaoh's daughter, "Shall I go and get one of the Hebrew women to nurse the baby for you?" "Yes, go," she answered. And the <u>girl</u> went and got the baby's mother. (Exodus 2:3-8 NLT)

... Israelites went through the <u>sea</u> on dry ground, with a wall of water on their right and on their left ... when the Israelites saw the great <u>power</u> the LORD displayed ... the people feared the LORD and put their <u>trust</u> in him and in Moses his servant. (Exodus 14:29, 31 NIV)

Then Miriam the <u>prophetess</u>, Aaron's sister, took a <u>tambourine</u> in her hand, and all the <u>women</u> followed her, with tambourines and <u>dancing</u>. Miriam sang to them:

"<u>Sing</u> to the LORD,
for he is highly exalted.
The <u>horse</u> and its <u>rider</u>
he has hurled into the sea." (Exodus 15:20-21 NIV)

... Miriam and Aaron spake against Moses because of the <u>Ethiopian</u> woman whom he had married ... Hath the LORD indeed spoken only by Moses? hath he not spoken also by us? (Numbers 12:1-2 KJV)

At once the LORD said to Moses, Aaron and Miriam, "Come out to the <u>Tent</u> of <u>Meeting</u>, all three of you." ... Then the LORD came down in a pillar of cloud; he stood at the <u>entrance</u> to the Tent ... When both of them <u>stepped</u> forward, he said, "Listen to my words:

"When a prophet of the LORD is among you, I <u>reveal</u> myself to him in visions, I speak to him in <u>dreams</u>. But this is not true of my servant Moses; he is faithful in all my house. With him I speak <u>face</u> to face, clearly and not in <u>riddles</u>; he sees the form of the LORD. Why then were you not <u>afraid</u> to speak against my servant Moses?" (Num. 12:4-8 NIV)

Bible Word Search, Vol. II: Women in the Bible

```
A S R Y G M E E T I N G V U S
B U V J F Z C G R I D D L E S
J C S Z O N N Q E E G O K Y E
V Z T C Y Q A U D N V L D L T
W D M T G I R S I S T E R V E
H P T A G R T C R O B I E X H
R W Y M F L N I L E G Z A E P
H T T B K A E R H C V V M X O
F D S O D I M C M O S E S O R
M E R U H N O R A A A S A B P
X P Q R R J W G V F I V E L O
E P S I E T G R R M A R M A W
O E L N D R N A U T X Z I O E
H T N E T H I O P I A N R M R
E S R O H D S T N E R A P R W
```

COPYRIGHT © GIL PUBLICATIONS 2006

22. Miriam

AARON	JOCHEBED	RIDDLES
AFRAID	LEVI	RIDER
AMRAM	MEETING	SEA
DANCING	MIRIAM	SING
DREAMS	MOSES	SISTER
ENTRANCE	NILE	STEPPED
ETHIOPIAN	PARENTS	TAMBOURINE
FACE	POWER	TENT
GIRL	PROPHETESS	TRUST
HORSE	REVEAL	WOMEN

GIL Publications, P. O. Box 80275, Brooklyn, NY 11208
www.BibleWordSearchPuzzles.com

23. Naomi

In the days when the <u>judges</u> ruled, there was a <u>famine</u> in the land, and a man from <u>Bethlehem</u> in Judah, together with his wife and two sons, went to live for a while in the country of <u>Moab</u>. The man's name was <u>Elimelech</u>, his wife's name <u>Naomi</u>, and the names of his two sons were <u>Mahlon</u> and <u>Kilion</u>. They were <u>Ephrathites</u> from Bethlehem, Judah. And they went to Moab and lived there. Now Elimelech, Naomi's husband, died, and she was left with her two sons. ⁴They married Moabite women, one named <u>Orpah</u> and the other <u>Ruth</u>. After they had lived there about ten years, both Mahlon and Kilion also died, and Naomi was left without her two sons and her husband...

When she heard in Moab that the LORD had come to the aid of his people by <u>providing</u> food for them, Naomi and her daughters-in-law <u>prepared</u> to <u>return</u> home from there. Then Naomi said to her two daughters-in-law, "Go back, each of you, to your mother's home. May the LORD show <u>kindness</u> to you, as you have shown to your dead and to me...

At this they <u>wept</u> again. Then Orpah kissed her mother-in-law good-by, but Ruth <u>clung</u> to her ... So the two women went on <u>until</u> they came to Bethlehem. When they arrived in Bethlehem, the whole town was <u>stirred</u> because of them, and the women exclaimed, "Can this be Naomi?"

"Don't call me Naomi," she told them. "Call me <u>Mara</u>, because the Almighty has made my life very <u>bitter</u>. I went away full, but the LORD has brought me back <u>empty</u>. Why call me Naomi? The LORD has afflicted me; the Almighty has brought <u>misfortune</u> upon me."

So Naomi returned from Moab accompanied by Ruth the Moabitess, her daughter-in-law, arriving in Bethlehem as the <u>barley</u> <u>harvest</u> was beginning...

Now Naomi had a relative on her husband's side, from the clan of Elimelech, a man of standing, whose name was <u>Boaz</u>...

Boaz replied, "I've been told all about what you have done for your mother-in-law since the <u>death</u> of your husband—how you left your father and mother and your homeland and came to live with a people you did not know before.

"The LORD bless him!" Naomi said to her daughter-in-law. "He has not stopped showing his kindness to the living and the dead." She added, "That man is our close relative; he is one of our <u>kinsman</u>-redeemers."

One day Naomi her mother-in-law said to her, "My daughter, should I not try to find a home for you, where you will be well provided for?

Stay here for the night, and in the morning if he wants to <u>redeem</u>, good; let him redeem. But if he is not willing, as <u>surely</u> as the LORD lives I will do it. Lie here until morning." ... When Ruth came to her mother-in-law, Naomi asked, "How did it go, my daughter?" ... Then she told him everything Boaz had done for her and added, "He gave me these six measures of barley, saying, 'Don't go back to your mother-in-law empty-handed.'"

(Ruth 1:1-8, 14, 19-22; 2:1, 11, 20; 3:1, 13, 16-17 NIV)

Bible Word Search, Vol. II: Women in the Bible

```
U E N U T R O F S I M E C N N
K I N D N E S S Y G Y W Q E E
F A M I N E L L E R U T H O I
X P R O V I D I N G V N P G H
N O L H A M P T M W D R N M S
K I L I O N L N O E A U Y C E
D I B O A Z O U A H L T J S T
E A N L R Z Q T B C N E U R I
R O B S A C H G S F B R C Z H
A Z I T M I H A R V E S T H T
P F E I N A P J W L O N M P A
E D T R F K N V Y E L R A B R
R C N R E T T I B Z P Z G O H
P S M E H E L H T E B T E V P
T R E D E E M K M H Q B P B E
```

COPYRIGHT © GIL PUBLICATIONS 2006

23. Naomi

- BARLEY
- BETHLEHEM
- BITTER
- BOAZ
- CLUNG
- DEATH
- ELIMELECH
- EMPTY
- EPHRATHITES
- FAMINE
- HARVEST
- JUDGES
- KILION
- KINDNESS
- KINSMAN
- MAHLON
- MARA
- MISFORTUNE
- MOAB
- NAOMI
- OPRAH
- PREPARED
- PROVIDING
- REDEEM
- RETURN
- RUTH
- STIRRED
- SURELY
- UNTIL
- WEPT

GIL Publications, P. O. Box 80275, Brooklyn, NY 11208
www.BibleWordSearchPuzzles.com

24. Pharaoh's Daughter

... one of <u>Pharaoh</u>'s daughters came <u>down</u> to <u>bathe</u> in the <u>river</u>, and her servant girls walked along the riverbank. When the <u>princess</u> saw the little <u>basket</u> among the <u>reeds</u>, she told one of her servant girls to get it for her. As the princess opened it, she found the <u>baby</u> boy. His <u>helpless</u> <u>cries</u> touched her heart. "He must be one of the Hebrew children," she said.

Then the baby's sister approached the princess. "Should I go and find one of the Hebrew women to <u>nurse</u> the baby for you?" she asked.

"Yes, do!" the princess replied. So the girl <u>rushed</u> home and called the baby's mother.

"Take this child home and nurse him for me," the princess told her. "I will pay you for your help." So the baby's mother took her baby home and nursed him.

Later, when he was older, the child's mother <u>brought</u> him back to the princess, who <u>adopted</u> him as her son. The princess <u>named</u> him <u>Moses</u>, for she said, "I <u>drew</u> him out of the water." (Exodus 2:5-10 NLT)

"At that time Moses was born, and he was no <u>ordinary</u> child. For three months he was <u>cared</u> for in his father's house. When he was placed <u>outside</u>, Pharaoh's daughter took him and brought him up as her own son. Moses was <u>educated</u> in all the <u>wisdom</u> of the <u>Egyptians</u> and was <u>powerful</u> in <u>speech</u> and <u>action</u>. (Acts 7:20-22 NIV)

By <u>faith</u> Moses, when he was come to years, <u>refused</u> to be called the son of Pharaoh's daughter; Choosing rather to suffer affliction with the people of God, than to <u>enjoy</u> the pleasures of sin for a <u>season</u>. (Hebrews 11:24-25 KJV)

Bible Word Search, Vol. II: Women in the Bible

24. Pharaoh's Daughter

- ACTION
- ADOPTED
- BABY
- BASKET
- BATHE
- BROUGHT
- CARED
- CRIES
- DOWN
- DREW
- EDUCATED
- EGYPTIANS
- ENJOY
- FAITH
- HELPLESS
- MOSES
- NAMED
- NURSE
- ORDINARY
- OUTSIDE
- PHARAOH
- POWERFUL
- PRINCESS
- REEDS
- REFUSED
- RIVER
- RUSHED
- SEASON
- SPEECH
- WISDOM

25. Potiphar's Wife

Now when <u>Joseph</u> arrived in <u>Egypt</u> with the <u>Ishmaelite</u> <u>traders</u>, he was <u>purchased</u> by <u>Potiphar</u>, a member of the <u>personal</u> <u>staff</u> of <u>Pharaoh</u>, the king of Egypt. Potiphar was the <u>captain</u> of the palace <u>guard</u>.

The LORD was with Joseph and <u>blessed</u> him greatly as he served in the home of his Egyptian master … Now Joseph was a very handsome and well-built young man. And about this time, Potiphar's wife began to <u>desire</u> him and <u>invited</u> him to <u>sleep</u> with her. But Joseph refused. "Look," he told her, "my <u>master</u> <u>trusts</u> me with everything in his entire household. No one here has more authority than I do! He has held back nothing from me except you, because you are his wife. How could I ever do such a wicked thing? It would be a great sin against God."

She kept putting <u>pressure</u> on him day after day, but he refused to sleep with her, and he kept out of her way as much as possible. One day, however, no one else was around when he was doing his work inside the house. She came and <u>grabbed</u> him by his <u>shirt</u>, demanding, "Sleep with me!" Joseph <u>tore</u> himself away, but as he did, his shirt came off. She was left holding it as he ran from the house.

When she saw that she had his shirt and that he had fled, she began <u>screaming</u>. Soon all the men around the place came running. "My husband has brought this <u>Hebrew</u> <u>slave</u> here to <u>insult</u> us!" she <u>sobbed</u>. "He tried to rape me, but I screamed. When he heard my loud cries, he ran and left his shirt behind with me."

She kept the shirt with her, and when her husband came home that night, she told him her story. "That Hebrew slave you've had around here tried to make a fool of me," she said. "I was saved only by my screams. He ran out, leaving his shirt behind!"

After hearing his wife's story, Potiphar was <u>furious</u>! He took Joseph and threw him into the <u>prison</u> where the king's prisoners were held. But the LORD was with Joseph there, too, and he granted Joseph favor with the <u>chief</u> <u>jailer</u> … (Genesis 639:1-2, 6-21 NLT)

Bible Word Search, Vol. II: Women in the Bible

25. Potiphar's Wife

BLESSED	INVITED	PURCHASED
CAPTAIN	ISHMAELITE	SCREAMING
CHIEF	JAILER	SHIRT
DESIRE	JOSEPH	SLAVE
EGYPT	MASTER	SLEEP
FURIOUS	PERSONAL	SOBBED
GRABBED	PHAROAH	STAFF
GUARD	POTIPHAR	TORE
HEBREW	PRESSURE	TRADERS
INSULT	PRISON	TRUSTS

26. Proverbs: Women, Wives, Mothers

King James Version
...Attend unto my <u>wisdom</u>, and bow thine <u>ear</u> to my understanding: Let thy <u>fountain</u> be blessed: and <u>rejoice</u> with the <u>wife</u> of thy youth. Let her be as the loving <u>hind</u> and pleasant <u>roe</u>; let her <u>breasts</u> satisfy thee at all times; and be thou ravished always with her <u>love</u>. (5:1, 18-19)
So he that goeth in to his neighbour's wife; whosoever toucheth her shall not be innocent. (6:29)
A <u>foolish</u> woman is <u>clamorous</u>: she is simple, and knoweth nothing. (9:13)
The <u>proverbs</u> of Solomon. A <u>wise</u> son maketh a glad <u>father</u>: but a foolish son is the heaviness of his mother. (10:1)
A <u>gracious</u> woman retaineth honour: and strong men retain <u>riches</u>. (11:6)
As a jewel of gold in a <u>swine</u>'s snout, so is a <u>fair</u> woman which is without discretion. (11:22)
A <u>virtuous</u> woman is a <u>crown</u> to her husband: but she that maketh ashamed is as rottenness in his <u>bones</u>. (12:4)
Every wise woman buildeth <u>her</u> house: but the foolish plucketh it down with her hands. (14:1)
A wise son maketh a glad father: but a foolish man despiseth his <u>mother</u>. (15:20)
A foolish son is the calamity of his father: and the contentions of a wife are a continual dropping. House and riches are the inheritance of fathers: and a <u>prudent</u> wife is from the LORD. (19:13-14)
It is better to dwell in the wilderness, than with a contentious and an angry woman. (21:19)
It is better to dwell in a corner of the <u>housetop</u>, than with a <u>brawling</u> woman in a wide house. (25:24)
A continual dropping in a very rainy day and a <u>contentious</u> woman are <u>alike</u>. (27:15)
The <u>rod</u> and reproof give wisdom: but a child left to himself bringeth his mother to shame. (29:15)
Who can find a virtuous <u>woman</u>? for her price is far above rubies. Favour is deceitful, and beauty is vain: but a woman that feareth the LORD, she shall be praised. (31:10, 30)

Bible Word Search, Vol. II: Women in the Bible

26. Proverbs: Women, Wives, Mothers

ALIKE	FOOLISH	REJOICE
BONES	FOUNTAIN	RICHES
BRAWLING	GRACIOUS	ROD
BREASTS	HER	ROE
CLAMOROUS	HIND	SWINE
CONTENTIOUS	HOUSETOP	VIRTUOUS
CROWN	LOVE	WIFE
EAR	MOTHER	WISDOM
FAIR	PROVERBS	WISE
FATHER	PRUDENT	WOMAN

27. Queen of Sheba

And when the <u>queen</u> of <u>Sheba</u> heard of the <u>fame</u> of <u>Solomon</u> concerning the name of the LORD, she came to <u>prove</u> him with <u>hard</u> <u>questions</u>.

And she came to Jerusalem with a very great <u>train</u>, with <u>camels</u> that bare <u>spices</u>, and very much <u>gold</u>, and precious <u>stones</u>: and when she was come to Solomon, she communed with him of all that was in her heart. And Solomon told her all her questions: there was not any thing <u>hid</u> from the king, which he told her not.

And when the queen of Sheba had seen all Solomon's <u>wisdom</u>, and the house that he had built,

And the <u>meat</u> of his table, and the sitting of his <u>servants</u>, and the attendance of his ministers, and their <u>apparel</u>, and his <u>cupbearers</u>, and his <u>ascent</u> by which he went up unto the house of the LORD; there was no more spirit in her.

And she said to the king, It was a true <u>report</u> that I heard in mine own land of thy acts and of thy wisdom.

Howbeit I believed not the words, until I came, and mine eyes had seen it: and, behold, the half was not told me: thy wisdom and prosperity exceedeth the fame which I heard.

Happy are thy men, happy are these thy servants, which stand continually before thee, and that <u>hear</u> thy wisdom.

Blessed be the LORD thy God, which delighted in thee, to set thee on the <u>throne</u> of Israel: because the LORD loved Israel for ever, therefore made he thee king, to do judgment and <u>justice</u>.

And she gave the king an hundred and twenty <u>talents</u> of gold, and of spices very great store, and precious stones: there came no more such abundance of spices as these ...

And the navy also of Hiram, that brought gold from <u>Ophir</u>, brought in from Ophir great plenty of <u>almug</u> <u>trees</u>, and precious stones. And the king made of the almug trees pillars for the house of the LORD, and for the king's house, <u>harps</u> also and psalteries for singers: there came no such almug trees, nor were seen unto this day.

And king Solomon gave unto the queen of Sheba all her desire, whatsoever she asked, beside that which Solomon gave her of his <u>royal</u> <u>bounty</u>. So she turned and went to her own country, she and her servants. (1 Kings 10:1-13 KJV)

Bible Word Search, Vol. II: Women in the Bible

```
H A R D T E V O R P M S H B K
R O Y A L N L F S O T T O S N
S T R E E S D P D O R U T E S
L O T N M M R S N O N N C T S
S E L V D A I E P T E I N Y F
A R R O H W S E Y L T A B T A
C S E A M L R P A S V F C O M
W A C R P O I T U R U L F R E
T S M E A P N J E G Q U E E N
M H E E N E A S I O F D N D S
E L R C L T B L P C P L I H R
A S R O I S X P M V A O A I I
T X T E N P H A U U V G R D H
P R A E H E S C D C G Y T S P
S H E B A S N O I T S E U Q O
```

COPYRIGHT © GIL PUBLICATIONS 2006

27. Queen of Sheba

ALMUG	HEAR	SERVANTS
APPAREL	HID	SHEBA
ASCENT	JUSTICE	SOLOMON
BOUNTY	MEAT	SPICES
CAMELS	OPHIR	STONES
CUPBEARERS	PROVE	TALENTS
FAME	QUEEN	THRONE
GOLD	QUESTIONS	TRAIN
HARD	REPORT	TREES
HARPS	ROYAL	WISDOM

GIL Publications, P. O. Box 80275, Brooklyn, NY 11208
www.BibleWordSearchPuzzles.com

28. Rachel

Laban had two daughters: ... the elder *was* Leah ... the younger *was* Rachel ... Rachel was beautiful and well favoured. Jacob loved Rachel ... served seven years for Rachel ... seemed unto him *but* a few days, for the love he had to her.

... in the morning, behold, it *was* Leah: and he said to Laban, What *is* this thou hast done unto me? did not I serve with thee for Rachel ... thou beguiled me? And Laban said, It must not be so done in our country, to give the younger before the firstborn. ... serve with me yet seven other years ... and he gave him Rachel his daughter to wife also.

And when the LORD saw that Leah *was* hated, he opened her womb: but Rachel *was* barren ... Rachel envied her sister; and said unto Jacob, Give me children, or else I die ...

And Bilhah [Rachel's handmaid] conceived and bare Jacob a son ... Dan ... became pregnant again ... a second son. Rachel named him Naphtali, for she said, "I have had an intense struggle with my sister, and I am winning!"

Then God remembered Rachel's plight and answered her prayers by giving her a child. And she named him Joseph, for she said, "May the LORD give me yet another son."

And Jacob began to notice a considerable cooling in Laban's attitude toward him. Then the LORD said to Jacob, "Return to the land of your father and grandfather and to your relatives there, and I will be with you."

At the time they left, Laban was some distance away, shearing his sheep. Rachel stole her father's household gods and took them with her.

But the previous night God had appeared to Laban in a dream. "Be careful about what you say to Jacob!" he was told.

So when Laban caught up with Jacob as he was camped in the hill country of Gilead ... "What do you mean by sneaking off like this ... Are my daughters prisoners, the plunder of war, that you have stolen them away like this?

Laban went first into Jacob's tent to search there, then into Leah's ... then ... the two concubines, but he didn't find the gods. Finally, he went into Rachel's tent. Rachel had taken the household gods and had stuffed them into her camel saddle, and now she was sitting on them. ... he couldn't find them. "Forgive my not getting up, Father," Rachel explained. "I'm having my monthly period." So despite his thorough search, Laban didn't find them.

And it came to pass, when she was in hard labour, that the midwife said unto her, Fear not; thou shalt have this son also. And it came to pass, as her soul was in departing, (for she died) that she called his name Benoni: but his father called him Benjamin. And Rachel died, and was buried in the way to Ephrath, which *is* Bethlehem.

Genesis 29:16-18, 20, 25-28, 31: 30:1-2, 5-8, 22, 24; 31: 2-3, 19, 24-26, 33-35; 35:17-19 KJV)

Bible Word Search, Vol. II: Women in the Bible

Copyright © GIL Publications 2006

28. Rachel

- BARREN
- BEAUTIFUL
- BEGUILED
- BENJAMIN
- BENONI
- BILHAH
- CAMEL
- CONCUBINES
- COOLING
- DAN
- DEPARTING
- ENVIED
- EPHRATH
- GILEAD
- GRANDFATHER
- INTENSE
- JOSEPH
- LABAN
- LEAH
- NAPHTALI
- PLIGHT
- PLUNDER
- PRISONERS
- RACHEL
- SADDLE
- SEARCH
- SNEAKING
- STUFFED
- WINNING
- WOMB

29. Rahab

Then <u>Joshua</u> son of <u>Nun</u> <u>secretly</u> sent two <u>spies</u> from <u>Shittim</u>. "Go, look over the land," he said, "especially <u>Jericho</u>." So they went and entered the house of a <u>prostitute</u> named <u>Rahab</u> and stayed there ... So the <u>king</u> of Jericho sent this message to Rahab: "Bring out the men ...But the woman had taken the two men and hidden them ...

Before the spies lay down for the night, she went up on the <u>roof</u> and said to them, "I know that the LORD has given this land to you and that a great fear of you has <u>fallen</u> on us, so that all who live in this <u>country</u> are melting in fear because of you. We have heard how the LORD dried up the water of the <u>Red Sea</u> for you when you came out of Egypt, and what you did to <u>Sihon</u> and <u>Og</u>, the two kings of the <u>Amorites</u> east of the Jordan, whom you completely <u>destroyed</u>. When we heard of it, our hearts melted and everyone's <u>courage</u> <u>failed</u> because of you, for the LORD your God is God in heaven above and on the earth below ... Give me a sure sign that you will spare the lives of my father and mother, my brothers and sisters, and all who belong to them, and that you will save us from death ..."

So she let them down by a <u>rope</u> through the <u>window</u>, for the house she lived in was part of the city <u>wall</u>. Now she had said to them, "Go to the hills so the <u>pursuers</u> will not find you. Hide yourselves there three days until they return, and then go on your way." The men said to her, "This <u>oath</u> you made us swear will not be binding on us unless, when we enter the land, you have tied this <u>scarlet</u> <u>cord</u> in the window through which you let us down, and unless you have brought your father and mother, your brothers and all your family into your house. "Agreed," she replied. "Let it be as you say." So she sent them away and they departed. And she tied the scarlet cord in the window. (Joshua 2:1-21 NIV)

And Joshua saved Rahab the <u>harlot</u> alive, and her father's household, and all that she had; and she dwelleth in Israel even unto this day; because she hid the <u>messengers</u>, which Joshua sent to spy out Jericho. (Joshua 6:27 KJV)

It was by <u>faith</u> that Rahab the prostitute did not die with all the others in her city who refused to obey God. For she had given a <u>friendly</u> welcome to the spies. (Hebrews 11:31 NLT)

Bible Word Search, Vol. II: Women in the Bible

```
D E S T R O Y E D U S R J O D
S F R I E N D L Y P A W F E U
R I K Q H T A O I H O A Y M J
S E H W A L L E A D U N I E C
E R D O I B S B N H E T R O P
B G E S N J D I S L T I U R W
F O A G E B W O L I C N O S D
Y A B R N A J A H H T S R R S
L Y I S U E F S O R T N O E E
T S T L C O S B Y I I U O U T
E C O O E A C S T F X N F S I
R G G K L D R U E C A U J R R
C N E M E R T L G M O I J U O
E I N H A E A F E V E R T P M
S K R O P E I H L T O J D H A
```

29. Rahab

AMORITES	JERICHO	REDSEA
CORD	JOSHUA	ROOF
COUNTRY	KING	ROPE
COURAGE	MESSENGERS	SCARLET
DESTROYED	NUN	SECRETLY
FAILED	OATH	SHITTIM
FAITH	OG	SIHON
FALLEN	PROSTITUTE	SPIES
FRIENDLY	PURSUERS	WALL
HARLOT	RAHAB	WINDOW

30. Rebekak

One day <u>Abraham</u> said to the man in <u>charge</u> of his household, who was his <u>oldest</u> servant, "...Go instead to my <u>homeland</u>, to my relatives, and find a wife there for my son <u>Isaac</u>." (Genesis 24:22, 4 NLT)

Before he had finished praying, <u>Rebekah</u> came out with her <u>jar</u> on her <u>shoulder</u>. She was the daughter of <u>Bethuel</u> son of <u>Milcah</u>, who was the wife of Abraham's brother <u>Nahor</u>. The girl was very beautiful, a virgin; no man had ever lain with her. She went down to the <u>spring</u>, filled her jar and came up again.

So he said, "I am Abraham's servant. The LORD has blessed my master abundantly, and he has become <u>wealthy</u>. He has given him sheep and cattle, silver and gold, <u>menservants</u> and maidservants, and camels and donkeys. ^{36}My master's wife Sarah has borne him a son in her old age, and he has given him everything he owns. And my master made me swear an oath, and said, 'You must not get a wife for my son from the daughters of the Canaanites, in whose land I live,

So they called Rebekah and asked her, "Will you go with this man?"

"I will go," she said.

So they sent their sister Rebekah on her way, along with her nurse and Abraham's servant and his men.

Rebekah also looked up and saw Isaac. She got down from her camel Isaac brought her into the tent of his mother Sarah, and he married Rebekah. So she became his wife, and he loved her; and Isaac was <u>comforted</u> after his mother's death. (Genesis 24:15-17, 34-37, 58-59, 64, 67 NIV)

And Isaac was <u>forty</u> years old when he took Rebekah to wife, the daughter of Bethuel the Syrian of <u>Padanaram</u>, the sister to Laban the Syrian. And Isaac entreated the LORD for his wife, because she *was* barren: and the LORD was entreated of him, and Rebekah his wife conceived. And the children <u>struggled</u> together within her; and she said, If *it be* so, why *am* I thus? And she went to inquire of the LORD. And the LORD said unto her, Two nations *are* in thy womb, and two manner of people shall be separated from thy <u>bowels</u>; and *the one* people shall be stronger than *the other* people; and the <u>elder</u> shall serve the younger. And when her days to be delivered were fulfilled, behold, *there were* <u>twins</u> in her womb. And the first came out red, all over like an <u>hairy</u> <u>garment</u>; and they called his name <u>Esau</u>. And after that came his brother out, and his hand took hold on Esau's heel; and his name was called Jacob: and Isaac *was* threescore years old when she bare them. And the boys grew: and Esau was a <u>cunning</u> <u>hunter</u>, a man of the <u>field</u>; and Jacob *was* a plain man, dwelling in tents. And Isaac loved Esau, because he did eat of *his* <u>venison</u>: but Rebekah <u>loved</u> <u>Jacob</u>. (Genesis 25:20-28 KJV)

Bible Word Search, Vol. II: Women in the Bible

30. Rebekak

ABRAHAM	GARMENT	NAHOR
BETHUEL	HAIRY	OLDEST
BOWELS	HOMELAND	PADANARAM
CHARGE	HUNTER	REBEKAH
COMFORTED	ISSAC	SHOULDER
CUNNING	JACOB	SPRING
ELDER	JAR	STRUGGLED
ESAU	LOVED	TWINS
FIELD	MENSERVANTS	VENISON
FORTY	MILCAH	WEALTHY

31. Rizpah

One day Ishbosheth, Saul's son, accused Abner of sleeping with one of his father's concubines, a woman named Rizpah. Abner became furious. (2 Samuel 3-8a NLT)
But he gave them Saul's two sons Armoni and Mephibosheth, whose mother was Rizpah daughter of Aiah. He also gave them the five sons of Saul's daughter Merab, the wife of Adriel son of Barzillai from Meholah. The men of Gibeon executed them on the mountain before the LORD. So all seven of them died together at the beginning of the barley harvest.

Then Rizpah, the mother of two of the men, spread sackcloth on a rock and stayed there the entire harvest season. She prevented vultures from tearing at their bodies during the day and stopped wild animals from eating them at night. When David learned what Rizpah, Saul's concubine, had done, he went to the people of Jabesh-gilead and asked for the bones of Saul and his son Jonathan. (When Saul and Jonathan had died in a battle with the Philistines, it was the people of Jabesh-gilead who had retrieved their bodies from the public square of the Philistine city of Beth-shan.) So David brought the bones of Saul and Jonathan, as well as the bones of the men the Gibeonites had executed. He buried them all in the tomb of Kish, Saul's father, at the town of Zela in the land of Benjamin. After that, God ended the famine in the land of Israel.
(2 Samuel 21:8-14 NLT)

Bible Word Search, Vol. II: Women in the Bible

31. Rizpah

ABNER	FURIOUS	RIZPAH
ADRIEL	GIBEON	ROCK
AIAH	ISHBOSHETH	SACKCLOTH
ANIMALS	JABESH	SLEEPING
ARMONI	KISH	SQUARE
BARZILLAI	MEHOLAH	STOPPED
BATTLE	MEPHIBOSHETH	TEARING
BONES	MERAB	VULTURES
EATING	NIGHT	WILD
EXECUTED	PUBLIC	ZELA

32. Ruth

And Elimelech Naomi's husband died; and she was left, and her two sons. And they took them wives of the women of Moab ... Orpah, and ... Ruth: and they dwelled there about ten years. And Mahlon and Chilion died also both of them; and the woman was left of her two sons and her husband.
... Orpah kissed her mother in law [goodbye]; but Ruth clave unto her.
So they two went until they came to Bethlehem ... all the city was moved about them ... Naomi had a kinsman of her husband's, a mighty man of wealth, of the family of Elimelech; and his name *was* Boaz.
And Boaz answered and said unto her [Ruth], It hath fully been showed me, all that thou hast done unto thy mother in law since the death of thine husband: and *how* thou hast left thy father and thy mother, and the land of thy nativity, and art come unto a people which thou knewest not heretofore.
... his heart was merry, he went to lie down at the end of the heap of corn: and she came softly, and uncovered his feet, and laid her down. And it came to pass at midnight, that the man was afraid, and turned himself: and, behold, a woman lay at his feet. And he said, Who *art* thou? And she answered, I *am* Ruth thine handmaid: spread therefore thy skirt over thine handmaid; for thou *art* a near kinsman. And he said, Blessed *be* thou of the LORD, my daughter: *for* thou hast showed more kindness in the latter end than at the beginning, inasmuch as thou followedst not young men, whether poor or rich. And now, my daughter, fear not; I will do to thee all that thou requirest: for all the city of my people doth know that thou *art* a virtuous woman. And now it is true that I *am thy* near kinsman: howbeit there is a kinsman nearer than I.
And Boaz said unto the elders, and *unto* all the people, Ye *are* witnesses this day, that I have bought all that *was* Elimelech's, and all that *was* Chilion's and Mahlon's, of the hand of Naomi. Moreover Ruth the Moabitess, the wife of Mahlon, have I purchased to be my wife, to raise up the name of the dead upon his inheritance, that the name of the dead be not cut off from among his brethren, and from the gate of his place: ye *are* witnesses this day. And all the people that *were* in the gate, and the elders, said, We *are* witnesses. The LORD make the woman that is come into thine house like Rachel and like Leah, which two did build the house of Israel: and do thou worthily in Ephratah, and be famous in Bethlehem: And let thy house be like the house of Pharez, whom Tamar bare unto Judah, of the seed which the LORD shall give thee of this young woman.
So Boaz took Ruth, and she was his wife: and when he went in unto her, the LORD gave her conception, and she bare a son.
And the women her neighbours gave it a name, saying, There is a son born to Naomi; and they called his name Obed: he *is* the father of Jesse, the father of David. (Ruth 1:3-5, 14, 19; 2:1, 11; 3:1, 6-12; 4:1, 9-13, 17 KJV)

Bible Word Search, Vol. II: Women in the Bible

```
E F A M I L Y P E S B J M U Y
B N O I T P E C N O C F V I Z
N A T I V I T Y E F O U N Y Q
F F D V L S K I R T R L P F U
P N W J R T I M D L N L F H G
X E E L I P S O C Y J Y R R D
X I L Y C V S A Y Y R H E I A
I G L D H P E N A R E Q V E C
Z H E C A C D L E A U A O B F
A B D H P U U M P I D S E Z X
O O T I R C A M R O F Y R P V
B U P L O H L E S S E J O I O
R R Y I L H S A W A E P M E Z
L S U O U T R I V I N D C D Q
A G N N K H T L A E W I R M Q
```

COPYRIGHT © GIL PUBLICATIONS 2006

32. Ruth

BOAZ	INASMUCH	OBED
CHILION	JESSE	ORPAH
CLAVE	KISSED	PEOPLE
CONCEPTION	LAY	REQUIREST
CORN	MAHLON	RICH
DAVID	MERRY	RUTH
DWELLED	MOREOVER	SKIRT
FAMILY	NAOMI	SOFTLY
FULLY	NATIVITY	VIRTUOUS
HEAP	NEIGHBOURS	WEALTH

GIL Publications, P. O. Box 80275, Brooklyn, NY 11208
www.BibleWordSearchPuzzles.com

33. Samson's Mother

A certain man of Zorah, named Manoah, from the clan of the Danites, had a wife who was sterile and remained childless. The angel of the LORD appeared to her and said, "You are sterile and childless, but you are going to conceive and have a son. Now see to it that you drink no wine or other fermented drink and that you do not eat anything unclean, because you will conceive and give birth to a son. No razor may be used on his head, because the boy is to be a Nazirite, set apart to God from birth, and he will begin the deliverance of Israel from the hands of the Philistines."

Then the woman went to her husband and told him, "A man of God came to me. He looked like an angel of God, very awesome. I didn't ask him where he came from, and he didn't tell me his name.

God heard Manoah, and the angel of God came again to the woman while she was out in the field; but her husband Manoah was not with her. The woman hurried to tell her husband, "He's here! The man who appeared to me the other day!"

Manoah got up and followed his wife. When he came to the man, he said, "Are you the one who talked to my wife?"

"I am," he said.

So Manoah asked him, "When your words are fulfilled, what is to be the rule for the boy's life and work?"

The angel of the LORD answered, "Your wife must do all that I have told her.

Then Manoah took a young goat, together with the grain offering, and sacrificed it on a rock to the LORD . And the LORD did an amazing thing while Manoah and his wife watched: As the flame blazed up from the altar toward heaven, the angel of the LORD ascended in the flame. Seeing this, Manoah and his wife fell with their faces to the ground.

The woman gave birth to a boy and named him Samson. He grew and the LORD blessed him ...(Judges 13:2-6, 9-13, 19-20, 24 NIV)

Bible Word Search, Vol. II: Women in the Bible

Copyright © GIL Publications 2006

33. Samson's Mother

ALTAR	FERMENTED	OFFERING
ANGEL	FIELD	RAZOR
APART	FULFILLED	RULE
AWESOME	GOAT	SAMSON
BEGIN	GRAIN	STERILE
BIRTH	GROUND	TALKED
CHILDLESS	HURRIED	UNCLEAN
CLAN	LIFE	WORK
DANITES	MANOAH	YOUNG
DELIVERANCE	NAZIRITE	ZORAH

GIL Publications, P. O. Box 80275, Brooklyn, NY 11208
www.BibleWordSearchPuzzles.com

34. Sarah

And God said unto <u>Abraham</u>, As for <u>Sarai</u> thy wife, thou shalt not call her name Sarai, but <u>Sarah</u> shall her <u>name</u> be. And I will bless her, and give thee a <u>son</u> also of her: yea, I will bless her, and she shall be *a mother* of <u>nations</u>; <u>kings</u> of <u>people</u> shall be of her. And God said, Sarah thy wife shall bear thee a son indeed; and thou shalt call his name <u>Isaac</u>: and I will establish my <u>covenant</u> with him for an everlasting covenant, *and* with his <u>seed</u> after him. And as for <u>Ishmael</u>, I have <u>heard</u> thee: Behold, I have blessed him, and will make him fruitful, and will multiply him exceedingly; <u>twelve</u> princes shall he <u>beget</u>, and I will make him a great nation. But my covenant will I establish with Isaac, which Sarah shall bear unto thee at this set time in the next year. (Genesis 17:15-16; 19-21 KJV)

"Where is your wife Sarah?" they asked him.
"There, in the <u>tent</u>," he said.
Then the LORD said, "I will surely return to you about this time next year, and Sarah your <u>wife</u> will have a son."
Now Sarah was listening at the entrance to the tent, which was behind him. Abraham and Sarah were already <u>old</u> and well advanced in years, and Sarah was past the <u>age</u> of <u>childbearing</u>. So Sarah <u>laughed</u> to herself as she thought, "After I am worn out and my master is old, will I now have this pleasure?"

And the LORD visited Sarah as he had said, and the LORD did unto Sarah as he had <u>spoken</u>. And Abraham <u>circumcised</u> his son Isaac being <u>eight</u> days old, as God had commanded him. And Abraham was an <u>hundred</u> years old, when his son Isaac was born unto him. Sarah lived to be a hundred and twenty-seven years old. She died at Kiriath Arba (that is, <u>Hebron</u>) in the land of <u>Canaan</u>, and Abraham went to <u>mourn</u> for Sarah and to <u>weep</u> over her. (Genesis 18:6-12; 21:1,4-5; 23:1 NIV)

Bible Word Search, Vol. II: Women in the Bible

```
O J E M L U P A C T N E T P N
J H L D U B N E M A N S N P C
O H P Q G E A G A O A N Y G I
Q B O C K K J N H W T S X G R
N W E O V V A O A E I H I N C
T I P I S C V S R E O F E I U
M S Y P K C B A B P N F E R M
E H F T T S A R A H S H W A C
F M H E B N A A E E J C Q E I
H A G O S G N I K A I F O B S
E E V L E W T B Y R S Q H D E
B L B D E G H U N D R E D L D
R D Y I D E H G U A L Y I I S
O O G L O V M I C V E I G H T
N R U O M K T N A N E V O C R
```

COPYRIGHT © GIL PUBLICATIONS 2006

34. Sarah

ABRAHAM	HUNDRED	PEOPLE
AGE	ISAAC	SARAH
BEGET	ISHMAEL	SARAI
CANAAN	KINGS	SEED
CHILDBEARING	LAUGHED	SON
CIRCUMCISED	MOTHER	SPOKEN
COVENANT	MOURN	TENT
EIGHT	NAME	TWELVE
HEARD	NATIONS	WEEP
HEBRON	OLD	WIFE

GIL Publications, P. O. Box 80275, Brooklyn, NY 11208
www.BibleWordSearchPuzzles.com

35. Solomon's Wives

Now King <u>Solomon</u> loved many <u>foreign</u> <u>women</u>. Besides Pharaoh's daughter, he married women from <u>Moab</u>, <u>Ammon</u>, <u>Edom</u>, <u>Sidon</u>, and from among the <u>Hittites</u>. The LORD had <u>clearly</u> <u>instructed</u> his people not to <u>intermarry</u> with those nations, because the women they married would lead them to worship their gods. Yet Solomon <u>insisted</u> on loving them <u>anyway</u>. He had <u>seven</u> hundred <u>wives</u> and three hundred <u>concubines</u>. And sure <u>enough</u>, they led his heart away from the LORD. In Solomon's old age, they turned his <u>heart</u> to worship their gods <u>instead</u> of trusting <u>only</u> in the LORD his God, as his father, David, had done. Solomon worshiped <u>Ashtoreth</u>, the <u>goddess</u> of the Sidonians, and <u>Molech</u>, the <u>detestable</u> god of the Ammonites. Thus, Solomon did what was <u>evil</u> in the LORD'S sight; he refused to follow the LORD completely, as his father, David, had done. On the Mount of <u>Olives</u>, east of Jerusalem, he even <u>built</u> a <u>shrine</u> for <u>Chemosh</u>, the detestable god of Moab, and another for Molech, the detestable god of the Ammonites. Solomon built such shrines for all his foreign wives to use for burning <u>incense</u> and sacrificing to their gods. (1Kings 11:1-8 NLT)

Bible Word Search, Vol. II: Women in the Bible

35. Solomon's Wives

AMMON	EVIL	MOAB
ANYWAY	FOREIGN	MOLECH
ASHTORETH	GODDESS	OLIVES
BUILT	HEART	ONLY
CHEMOSH	HITTITES	SEVEN
CLEARLY	INCENSE	SHRINE
CONCUBINES	INSISTED	SIDOM
DETESTABLE	INSTEAD	SOLOMON
EDOM	INSTRUCTED	WIVES
ENOUGH	INTERMARRY	WOMEN

36. Tamar

<u>David</u>'s son <u>Absalom</u> had a beautiful sister named <u>Tamar</u>. And <u>Amnon</u>, her <u>half</u> brother, fell <u>desperately</u> in love with her. Amnon became so <u>obsessed</u> with Tamar that he became <u>ill</u>. She was a <u>virgin</u>, and it seemed <u>impossible</u> that he could ever fulfill his love for her.

Now Amnon had a very <u>crafty</u> <u>friend</u>—his <u>cousin</u> Jonadab. He was the son of David's brother <u>Shimea</u>. One day Jonadab said to Amnon, "What's the trouble? Why should the son of a king look so <u>dejected</u> morning after morning?" So Amnon told him, "I am in love with Tamar, Absalom's sister."

"Well," Jonadab said, "I'll tell you what to do. Go back to bed and <u>pretend</u> you are <u>sick</u>. When your father comes to see you, ask him to let Tamar come and prepare some food for you. Tell him you'll feel better if she feeds you."

When Tamar arrived at Amnon's house, she went to the <u>room</u> where he was <u>lying</u> down so he could watch her mix some <u>dough</u>. Then she baked some special bread for him. But when she set the serving tray before him, he refused to eat. "Everyone get out of here," Amnon told his servants. So they all left. Then he said to Tamar, "Now bring the food into my bedroom and feed it to me here." So Tamar took it to him. But as she was feeding him, he <u>grabbed</u> her and demanded, "Come to bed with me, my darling sister."

"No, my brother!" she cried. "Don't be foolish! Don't do this to me! You know what a <u>serious</u> <u>crime</u> it is to do such a thing in Israel. Where could I go in my shame? And you would be called one of the greatest fools in Israel. Please, just speak to the king about it, and he will let you marry me."

But Amnon wouldn't listen to her, and since he was <u>stronger</u> than she was, he raped her. Suddenly Amnon's love turned to <u>hate</u>, and he hated her even more than he had loved her. "Get out of here!" he snarled at her.

"No, no!" Tamar cried. "To reject me now is a greater <u>wrong</u> than what you have already done to me."

Absalom told his men, "Wait until Amnon gets drunk; then at my signal, kill him! Don't be afraid. I'm the one who has given the command. Take courage and do it!" So at Absalom's signal they murdered Amnon. Then the other sons of the king jumped on their <u>mules</u> and <u>fled</u>.

Absalom fled to his grandfather, Talmai son of Ammihud, the king of Geshur. He stayed there in Geshur for three years. And David, now reconciled to Amnon's death, longed to be <u>reunited</u> with his son Absalom.

(1 Samuel 13:1-5, 8-16, 28-29, 37-39 NLT)

Bible Word Search, Vol. II: Women in the Bible

```
D A V I D E S P E R A T E L Y
H B S I C K P B L O O A W Y T
K S G K R H C A J D N E I R F
R A M A T G R D B C H M R C A
F L A H L L I A I G N I Y L R
C O U S I N M N U G T H T F C
W M X P M T E O P N F S J L A
M R B A P B D J O O E R P E Z
R E G N O R T S O R T H R D O
M U L E S E U E I W A Y E E L
B N E P S G U O M S H K T B N
G I Z Z I G U Z D E S S E B O
L T C I B S F I I Y E B N A N
G E S K L R O S W Y S D D R M
T D K D E J E C T E D Q Z G A
```

COPYRIGHT © GIL PUBLICATIONS 2006

36. Tamar

ABSALOM	FRIEND	PRETEND
AMNON	GRABBED	REUNITED
COUSIN	HALF	ROOM
CRAFTY	HATE	SERIOUS
CRIME	ILL	SHIMEA
DAVID	IMPOSSIBLE	SICK
DEJECTED	JONADAB	STRONGER
DESPERATELY	LYING	TAMAR
DOUGH	MULES	VIRGIN
FLED	OBESSED	WRONG

GIL Publications, P. O. Box 80275, Brooklyn, NY 11208
www.BibleWordSearchPuzzles.com

37. Two Harlot Mothers (with Solomon)

Now two prostitutes [harlots - KJV] came to the king and stood before him. One of them said, "My lord, this woman and I live in the same house. I had a baby while she was there with me. The third day after my child was born, this woman also had a baby. We were alone; there was no one in the house but the two of us.

"During the night this woman's son died because she lay on him. So she got up in the middle of the night and took my son from my side while I your servant was asleep. She put him by her breast and put her dead son by my breast. The next morning, I got up to nurse my son-and he was dead! But when I looked at him closely in the morning light, I saw that it wasn't the son I had borne."

The other woman said, "No! The living one is my son; the dead one is yours."

But the first one insisted, "No! The dead one is yours; the living one is mine." And so they argued before the king.

The king said, "This one says, 'My son is alive and your son is dead,' while that one says, 'No! Your son is dead and mine is alive.' "

Then the king said, "Bring me a sword." So they brought a sword for the king. He then gave an order: "Cut the living child in two and give half to one and half to the other."

The woman whose son was alive was filled with compassion for her son and said to the king, "Please, my lord, give her the living baby! Don't kill him!"

But the other said, "Neither I nor you shall have him. Cut him in two!"

Then the king gave his ruling: "Give the living baby to the first woman. Do not kill him; she is his mother."

When all Israel heard the verdict the king had given, they held the king in awe, because they saw that he had wisdom from God to administer justice. (1 Kings 3:16-28 NIV)

Bible Word Search, Vol. II: Women in the Bible

37. Two harlots with Solomon

- ADMINISTER
- ALONE
- ARGUED
- ASLEEP
- AWE
- BABY
- BEFORE
- BREAST
- BROUGHT
- CHILD
- COMPASSION
- CUT
- DEAD
- FILLED
- HARLOTS
- INSISTED
- JUSTICE
- LIVING
- LOOKED
- MIDDLE
- MORNING
- MOTHER
- NIGHT
- NURSE
- ORDER
- PLEASE
- PROSTITUTES
- SWORD
- WISDOM
- WOMAN

38. Vashti

Now it came to pass in the days of <u>Ahasuerus</u>, (this *is* Ahasuerus which <u>reigned</u>, from <u>India</u> even unto <u>Ethiopia</u>, *over* an hundred and seven and twenty provinces:) ... In the third year of his reign, he made a feast unto all his princes and his servants; the power of <u>Persia</u> and <u>Media</u>, the <u>nobles</u> and princes of the <u>provinces</u>, *being* before him: When he showed the riches of his glorious kingdom and the honour of his excellent majesty many days, *even* an hundred and fourscore days. And when these days were expired, the king made a feast unto all the people that were present in <u>Shushan</u> the palace, both unto great and small, seven days, in the court of the <u>garden</u> of the king's palace;

And they gave *them* drink in <u>vessels</u> of gold, (the vessels being diverse one from another,) and royal wine in abundance, according to the <u>state</u> of the king. And the drinking *was* according to the law; none did <u>compel</u>: for so the king had appointed to all the officers of his house, that they should do according to every man's pleasure. Also <u>Vashti</u> the queen made a feast for the women *in* the royal house which *belonged* to king Ahasuerus.

On the seventh day, when the heart of the king was merry with wine, he commanded <u>Mehuman</u>, <u>Biztha</u>, <u>Harbona</u>, <u>Bigtha</u>, and <u>Abagtha</u>, <u>Zethar</u>, and <u>Carcas</u>, the seven chamberlains that served in the presence of Ahasuerus the king, To bring Vashti the queen before the king with the crown royal, to show the people and the princes her <u>beauty</u>: for she *was* fair to look on. For *this* deed of the queen shall come abroad unto all women, so that they shall despise their husbands in their eyes, when it shall be reported, The king Ahasuerus commanded Vashti the queen to be brought in before him, but she came not. *Likewise* shall the ladies of Persia and Media say this day unto all the king's princes, which have heard of the <u>deed</u> of the queen. Thus *shall there arise* too much <u>contempt</u> and <u>wrath</u>. If it please the king, let there go a royal commandment from him, and let it be written among the laws of the Persians and the Medes, that it be not <u>altered</u>, That Vashti come no more before king Ahasuerus; and let the king give her royal estate unto another that is better than she.

After these things, when the wrath of king Ahasuerus was <u>appeased</u>, he remembered Vashti, and what she had done, and what was <u>decreed</u> against her. Then said the king's servants that ministered unto him, Let there be fair young virgins sought for the king: And let the maiden which pleaseth the king be <u>queen</u> instead of Vashti. And the thing pleased the king; and he did so.

And he brought up Hadassah, that *is*, Esther, his uncle's daughter: for she had neither father nor mother, and the maid *was* fair and beautiful; whom <u>Mordecai</u>, when her father and mother were dead, took for his own daughter. (Esther 1:1, 3-5, 7-12, 17-19; 2:1-2, 4, 7 KJV)

38. Vahti

ABAGTHA	DECREED	PERSIA
AHASUERUS	DEED	PROVINCES
ALTERED	ETHIOPIA	QUEEN
APPEASED	GARDEN	REIGNED
BEAUTY	HARBONA	SHUSHAN
BIGTHA	INDIA	STATE
BIZTHA	MEDIA	VASHTI
CARCAS	MEHUMAN	VESSELS
COMPEL	MORDECAI	WRATH
CONTEMPT	NOBLES	ZETHAR

39. The Widow at Zarephath

And the word of the LORD came unto him, saying, Arise, get thee to <u>Zarephath</u>, which belongeth to <u>Zidon</u>, and dwell there: behold, I have commanded a <u>widow</u> woman there to <u>sustain</u> thee.

So he <u>arose</u> and went to Zarephath. And when he came to the gate of the city, behold, the widow woman was there gathering of <u>sticks</u>: and he called to her, and said, <u>Fetch</u> me, I pray thee, a little water in a <u>vessel</u>, that I may <u>drink</u>. And as she was going to fetch it, he called to her, and said, Bring me, I pray thee, a <u>morsel</u> of <u>bread</u> in thine hand.

And she said, As the LORD thy God liveth, I have not a <u>cake</u>, but an handful of <u>meal</u> in a <u>barrel</u>, and a little <u>oil</u> in a <u>cruse</u>: and, behold, I am gathering two sticks, that I may go in and <u>dress</u> it for me and my son, that we may eat it, and <u>die</u>. And <u>Elijah</u> said unto her, Fear not; go and do as thou hast said: but make me thereof a little cake first, and bring it unto me, and after make for thee and for thy son.

For thus saith the LORD God of Israel, The barrel of meal shall not <u>waste</u>, neither shall the cruse of oil <u>fail</u>, until the day that the LORD sendeth <u>rain</u> upon the earth.

And she went and did according to the saying of Elijah: and she, and he, and her house, did eat many days ... And it came to pass after these things, that the son of the woman, the mistress of the house, fell <u>sick</u>; and his sickness was so <u>sore</u>, that there was no breath left in him.

And she said unto Elijah, What have I to do with thee, O thou man of God? art thou come unto me to call my sin to remembrance, and to <u>slay</u> my son? And he said unto her, Give me thy son. And he took him out of her <u>bosom</u>, and carried him up into a loft, where he <u>abode</u>, and laid him upon his own bed.

And he cried unto the LORD, and said, O LORD my God, hast thou also brought evil upon the widow with whom I <u>sojourn</u>, by slaying her son?

And he stretched himself upon the child <u>three</u> times, and cried unto the LORD, and said, O LORD my God, I pray thee, let this child's soul come into him again.

And the LORD heard the voice of Elijah; and the soul of the child came into him again, and he <u>revived</u>. And Elijah took the child, and brought him down out of the chamber into the house, and delivered him unto his mother: and Elijah said, See, thy son liveth.

And the woman said to Elijah, Now by this I know that thou art a man of God, and that the word of the LORD in thy mouth is truth. (I Kings 17:8-24 KJV)

Bible Word Search, Vol. II: Women in the Bible

```
W Z E E A L N R W P E O H I Q
I K F B E R E M M S R J O A X
S C O R U V K B U Y E A N N J
I D R O I M S R R D H T E B L
E A J V O S C T Q E R C S B I
B O E R M F U S I V A E T A O
S D S O K A Z S H C E D S E W
Z E S N E I S A T H K S D S F
L O I E I L R R A A S O X Z
B R R Z J Y A I L E I J S R E
D H M E A L Y G F H P N I L A
T D I E L V E E K A C H X L T
Z I D O N S O R E S R J A W E
R A I N R Y H Q W O D I W T Y
V E S S E L W L M D K C I S H
```

COPYRIGHT © GIL PUBLICATIONS 2006

39. The Widow of Zarephath

ABODE	ELIJAH	SOJOURN
AROSE	FAIL	SORE
BARREL	FETCH	STICKS
BOSOM	MEAL	SUSTAIN
BREAD	MORSEL	THREE
CAKE	OIL	VESSEL
CRUSE	RAIN	WASTE
DIE	REVIVED	WIDOW
DRESS	SICK	ZAREPHATH
DRINK	SLAY	ZIDON

GIL Publications, P. O. Box 80275, Brooklyn, NY 11208
www.BibleWordSearchPuzzles.com

40. Widow's Oil

The wife of a man from the <u>company</u> of the <u>prophets</u> <u>cried</u> out to <u>Elisha</u>, "Your <u>servant</u> my husband is <u>dead</u>, and you know that he <u>revered</u> the LORD. But now his creditor is coming to take my two <u>boys</u> as his <u>slaves</u>."

Elisha replied to her, "How can I help you? Tell me, what do you have in your house?"

"Your servant has <u>nothing</u> there at all," she said, "<u>except</u> a little oil."

Elisha said, "Go around and ask all your <u>neighbors</u> for <u>empty</u> <u>jars</u>. Don't ask for just a <u>few</u>. Then go <u>inside</u> and <u>shut</u> the <u>door</u> behind you and your sons. Pour <u>oil</u> into all the jars, and as each is <u>filled</u>, put it to one side."

She left him and afterward shut the door behind her and her sons. They brought the jars to her and she <u>kept</u> <u>pouring</u>. When all the jars were <u>full</u>, she said to her son, "Bring me another one."

But he replied, "There is not a jar left." Then the oil <u>stopped</u> <u>flowing</u>.

She went and told the man of God, and he said, "Go, sell the oil and <u>pay</u> <u>your</u> <u>debts</u>. You and your sons can <u>live</u> on what is <u>left</u>." (2 Kings 4:1-7 NIV)

Bible Word Search, Vol. II: Women in the Bible

```
K F A A D G T G I D Y D L Z H
X N T E E N N G N N E T A S G
I J B L A I N E S T S I P E G
N T A V R I I N D T P I R M D
S V R U W G P C O E O E D C E
C E O O H D R S O T R P C E W
S P L B E S O A O M H E P X J
P F O L E K P H I I P I V E E
N R L V L A H S L Q H A N E D
S I A B V V E I Y A P W N G R
F L U Q O L T L R U O Y V Y R
S V P U A Y S E V T F E L I O
V V E T E K S W E F T P E K O
F U L L L I V E N P Y D Z Z D
S H U T I Q O C F Q I S R A J
```

COPYRIGHT © GIL PUBLICATIONS 2006

40. Widow's Oil

BOYS	FILLED	OIL
COMPANY	FLOWING	PAY
CRIED	FULL	POURING
DEAD	INSIDE	PROPHETS
DEBTS	JARS	REVERED
DOOR	KEPT	SERVANT
ELISHA	LEFT	SHUT
EMPTY	LIVE	SLAVES
EXCEPT	NEIGHBORS	STOPPED
FEW	NOTHING	YOUR

GIL Publications, P. O. Box 80275, Brooklyn, NY 11208
www.BibleWordSearchPuzzles.com

41. Wise Woman of Abel

2 Samuel 20:16-22 NLT

Then cried a wise woman out of the city, Hear, hear; say, I pray you, unto Joab, Come near hither, that I may speak with thee. And when he was come near unto her, the woman said, *Art* thou Joab? And he answered, I *am* he. Then she said unto him, Hear the words of thine handmaid. And he answered, I do hear. Then she spake, saying, They were wont to speak in old time, saying, They shall surely ask counsel at Abel: and so they ended the matter. I *am one of them that are* peaceable *and* faithful in Israel: thou seekest to destroy a city and a mother in Israel: why wilt thou swallow up the inheritance of the LORD? And Joab answered and said, Far be it, far be it from me, that I should swallow up or destroy. The matter *is* not so: but a man of mount Ephraim, Sheba the son of Bichri by name, hath lifted up his hand against the king, *even* against David: deliver him only, and I will depart from the city. And the woman said unto Joab, Behold, his head shall be thrown to thee over the wall. Then the woman went unto all the people in her wisdom. And they cut off the head of Sheba the son of Bichri, and cast *it* out to Joab. And he blew a trumpet, and they retired from the city, every man to his tent. And Joab returned to Jerusalem unto the king. (KJV)

But a wise woman in the city called out to Joab, "Listen to me, Joab. Come over here so I can talk to you." As he approached, the woman asked, "Are you Joab?"
"I am," he replied.
So she said, "Listen carefully to your servant."
"I'm listening," he said.
Then she continued, "There used to be a saying, 'If you want to settle an argument, ask advice at the city of Abel.' I am one who is peace loving and faithful in Israel. But you are destroying a loyal city. Why do you want to destroy what belongs to the LORD?"
And Joab replied, "Believe me, I don't want to destroy your city! All I want is a man named Sheba son of Bicri from the hill country of Ephraim, who has revolted against King David. If you hand him over to me, we will leave the city in peace."
"All right," the woman replied, "we will throw his head over the wall to you." Then the woman went to the people with her wise advice, and they cut off Sheba's head and threw it out to Joab. So he blew the trumpet and called his troops back from the attack, and they all returned to their homes. Joab returned to the king at Jerusalem. (NLT)

Bible Word Search, Vol. II: Women in the Bible

41. Wise Woman of Abel

ABEL	DESTROY	REVOLTED
AGAINST	ENDED	SEEKEST
APPROACHED	EPHRAIM	SETTLE
ARGUMENT	HANDMAID	SHEBA
ATTACK	HITHER	SPAKE
BELONGS	JOAB	SWALLOW
BICHRI	LEAVE	THROWN
BICRI	LIFTED	TROOPS
COUNSEL	LOVING	TRUMPET
DELIVER	MOUNT	WISDOM

GIL Publications, P. O. Box 80275, Brooklyn, NY 11208
www.BibleWordSearchPuzzles.com

42. Woman of Thebez

Next Abimelech went to Thebez and besieged it and captured it. Inside the city, however, was a strong tower, to which all the men and women-all the people of the city-fled. They locked themselves in and climbed up on the tower roof. Abimelech went to the tower and stormed it. But as he approached the entrance to the tower to set it on fire, a woman dropped an upper millstone on his head and cracked his skull.

Hurriedly he called to his armor-bearer, "Draw your sword and kill me, so that they can't say, 'A woman killed him.'" So his servant ran him through, and he died. When the Israelites saw that Abimelech was dead, they went home.

Thus God repaid the wickedness that Abimelech had done to his father by murdering his seventy brothers. God also made the men of Shechem pay for all their wickedness. The curse of Jotham son of Jerub-Baal came on them. (Judges 9:50-57 NIV)

Bible Word Search, Vol. II: Women in the Bible

```
Z V W V S S E N D E K C I W N
J M H M E H C E H S N K D X J
O Q D G K M U R D E R I N G E
T V H D C B A A L V C N I V R
H D V E A Y R D C E U E V D U
A N T G P E T E L N R C D R B
M E H E T D O K I T S N D O M
V X E I U I W C M Y E A R P I
D T B S R S E O B N R R E P L
I C E E E N R L E A O T P E L
A E Z B D I Y V D R O N P D S
P A M H C D R O W S F E U B T
E K E M O H I D M S E R I F O
R B E A R E R S K U L L D L N
A R M O R V W D E K C A R C E
```

Copyright © GIL Publications 2006

42. Woman of Thebez

ARMOR	FIRE	REPAID
BAAL	HOME	ROOF
BEARER	INSIDE	SEVENTY
BESIEGED	JERUB	SHECHEM
CAPTURED	JOTHAM	SKULL
CLIMBED	LOCKED	SWORD
CRACKED	MILLSTONE	THEBEZ
CURSE	MURDERING	TOWER
DROPPED	NEXT	UPPER
ENTRANCE	RAN	WICKEDNESS

GIL Publications, P. O. Box 80275, Brooklyn, NY 11208
www.BibleWordSearchPuzzles.com

43. Woman with Familiar Spirit at Endor

Now <u>Samuel</u> was dead, and all Israel had <u>mourned</u> for him and <u>buried</u> him in his own town of Ramah. Saul had <u>expelled</u> the <u>mediums</u> and <u>spiritists</u> from the land ...

When <u>Saul</u> saw the Philistine army, he was afraid; <u>terror</u> filled his heart. He <u>inquired</u> of the LORD , but the LORD did not <u>answer</u> him by <u>dreams</u> or <u>Urim</u> or <u>prophets</u>. Saul then said to his attendants, "Find me a woman who is a medium, so I may go and inquire of her."

"There is one in <u>Endor</u>," they said.

So Saul <u>disguised</u> himself, putting on other clothes, and at night he and two men went to the woman. "<u>Consult</u> a spirit for me," he said, "and bring up for me the one I name."

But the woman said to him, "Surely you know what Saul has done. He has cut off the mediums and spiritists from the land. Why have you set a trap for my life to bring about my death?"

Saul <u>swore</u> to her by the LORD , "As surely as the LORD lives, you will not be punished for this."

Then the woman asked, "Whom shall I bring up for you?"

"Bring up Samuel," he said.

Samuel said, "Why do you consult me, now that the LORD has turned away from you and become your <u>enemy</u>? The LORD has done what he <u>predicted</u> through me. The LORD has <u>torn</u> the kingdom out of your hands and given it to one of your neighbors-to David. Because you did not obey the LORD or carry out his <u>fierce</u> wrath against the <u>Amalekites</u>, the LORD has done this to you today. The LORD will hand over both Israel and you to the Philistines, and tomorrow you and your sons will be with me. The LORD will also hand over the army of Israel to the Philistines."

Immediately Saul fell full <u>length</u> on the ground, filled with fear because of Samuel's words. His strength was gone, for he had eaten nothing all that day and night.

When the woman came to Saul and saw that he was greatly <u>shaken</u>, she said, "Look, your maidservant has obeyed you. I took my life in my hands and did what you told me to do. Now please listen to your servant and let me give you some food so you may eat and have the strength to go on your way."

He refused and said, "I will not eat." But his men <u>joined</u> the woman in <u>urging</u> him ... He got up from the ground and sat on the <u>couch</u>.

The woman had a fattened <u>calf</u> at the house, which she butchered at once. She took some flour, <u>kneaded</u> it and <u>baked</u> bread without yeast. Then she set it before Saul and his men, and they ate. That same night they got up and left. (1 Samuel 28: 3, 5-11, 16-25 NIV)

Bible Word Search, Vol. II: Women in the Bible

```
D E R I U Q N I G S W O R E W
T J L E T Y M E N E E H Q V M
E P V U K B U R I E D T O R N
R G S H A K E N G W J G U S E
R E B A N S W E R R P N T P P
O D S V D I S G U I S E D I R
R R E E C R E I F R H L M R E
A E K L S M T M R P P J E I D
H A D T L U S N O C N N D T I
B M E R L E Q R O D N E I I C
C S N H W J P Q Z V D Y U S T
Z U R I M F V X K A A V M T E
H C U O C A L F E C P Q S S D
C J O I N E D N L S A M U E L
Q A M A L E K I T E S T I I C
```

COPYRIGHT © GIL PUBLICATIONS 2006

43. Woman with Familiar Spirit at Endor

AMALEKITES	ENEMY	PROPHETS
ANSWER	EXPELLED	SAMUEL
BAKED	FIERCE	SAUL
BURIED	INQUIRED	SHAKEN
CALF	JOINED	SPIRITISTS
CONSULT	KNEADED	SWORE
COUCH	LENGTH	TERROR
DISGUISED	MEDIUMS	TORN
DREAMS	MOURNED	URGING
ENDOR	PREDICTED	URIM

GIL Publications, P. O. Box 80275, Brooklyn, NY 11208
www.BibleWordSearchPuzzles.com

44. Zipporah (Moses' Wife)

Now a priest of Midian had seven daughters, and they came to draw water and fill the troughs to water their father's flock. Some shepherds came along and drove them away, but Moses got up and came to their rescue and watered their flock.

When the girls returned to Reuel their father, he asked them, "Why have you returned so early today?"

They answered, "An Egyptian rescued us from the shepherds. He even drew water for us and watered the flock."

"And where is he?" he asked his daughters. "Why did you leave him? Invite him to have something to eat."

Moses agreed to stay with the man, who gave his daughter Zipporah to Moses in marriage. Zipporah gave birth to a son, and Moses named him Gershom, saying, "I have become an alien in a foreign land." (Exodus 2:16-22 NIV)

At a lodging place on the way, the LORD met {Moses} and was about to kill him. But Zipporah took a flint knife, cut off her son's foreskin and touched {Moses'} feet with it. "Surely you are a bridegroom of blood to me," she said. So the LORD let him alone. (At that time she said "bridegroom of blood," referring to circumcision.) (Exodus 4:24-26 NIV)

Now Jethro, the priest of Midian and father-in-law of Moses, heard of everything God had done for Moses and for his people Israel, and how the LORD had brought Israel out of Egypt.

After Moses had sent away his wife Zipporah, his father-in-law Jethro received her and her two sons. One son was named Gershom, for Moses said, "I have become an alien in a foreign land"; and the other was named Eliezer, for he said, "My father's God was my helper; he saved me from the sword of Pharaoh." Jethro, Moses' father-in-law, together with Moses' sons and wife, came to him in the desert, where he was camped near the mountain of God. Jethro had sent word to him, "I, your father-in-law Jethro, am coming to you with your wife and her two sons." (Exodus 4:1-6 NIV)

Bible Word Search, Vol. II: Women in the Bible

```
G T A C G H T N I L F E N E J
M E R L P L E U E R A A L C L
Y O R E I W I F E R I I I O T
G K O S S E E V L D E R D O R
H N Y R H E N Y I Z C G D U O
A I Y Y G O D M E U I Y R S U
R F A D P E M R M N L U A E G
O E D N I E D C G T E Q W S H
P V O E U L I I H O S G N O S
P K T C E S C U R O R E Y M I
I X S A I A D P Z B A H I P J
Z E R O M F D R O W S R T R T
R S N P F L O C K P E B A E P
I E E D D E G A I R R A M H J
R D F O R E S K I N C U T Z P
```

COPYRIGHT © GIL PUBLICATIONS 2006

44. Zipporah (Moses' Wife)

ALIEN	FLINT	MOSES
BRIDEGROOM	FLOCK	PHARAOH
CAMPED	FORESKIN	PRIEST
CIRCUMCISION	GERSHOM	RESCUE
CUT	ISRAEL	REUEL
DESERT	JETHRO	SWORD
DRAW	KNIFE	TODAY
EARLY	LODGING	TROUGHS
EGYPT	MARRIAGE	WIFE
ELIEZER	MIDIAN	ZIPPORAH

GIL Publications, P. O. Box 80275, Brooklyn, NY 11208
www.BibleWordSearchPuzzles.com

45. A Woman's Beauty Is Measured By

<u>Favour</u> is deceitful, and beauty is <u>vain</u>: but a woman that feareth the LORD, she shall be praised. (Proverbs 31:30 KJV)

Don't be concerned about the <u>outward</u> beauty that depends on <u>fancy</u> <u>hairstyles</u>, <u>expensive</u> <u>jewelry</u>, or beautiful <u>clothes</u>. You should be known for the beauty that <u>comes</u> from <u>within</u>, the unfading beauty of a <u>gentle</u> and <u>quiet</u> <u>spirit</u>, which is so <u>precious</u> to God. That is the way the <u>holy</u> women of old made themselves <u>beautiful</u>. (1 Peter 3:3-5 NLT)

In like <u>manner</u> also, that women <u>adorn</u> themselves in <u>modest</u> <u>apparel</u>, with shamefacedness and <u>sobriety</u>; not with broided hair, or <u>gold</u>, or <u>pearls</u>, or costly <u>array</u>; But (which becometh women professing <u>godliness</u>) with good works. (1 Timothy 2:9-10 KJV)

And I want women to be modest in their appearance. They should wear <u>decent</u> and appropriate clothing and not draw attention to themselves by the way they <u>fix</u> their <u>hair</u> or by wearing gold or pearls or expensive clothes. For women who claim to be <u>devoted</u> to God should make themselves attractive by the <u>good</u> things they do. (1 Timothy 2:9-10 NLT)

Bible Word Search, Vol. II: Women in the Bible

```
J N I R I X B J V D V Q P L O
G P G X M W Q Y F O D E Y S U
E S O B R I E T Y S O P S N T
M O D E S T D U C O M E S M W
G O L D V H Y A R R A W E N A
H A I R F I X E W M N C L Y R
F L N G Q N R B F A N C Y D D
O B E A U T I F U L E I T E Y
O D S P I R I T Y O R I S T R
G F S P E A R L S D W H R O L
V A I N T V E X P E N S I V E
Q V H S E H T O L C N U A E W
N O O I S U O I C E R P H D E
Y U L E R A P P A N R O D A J
V R Y U Q F G E N T L E J L X
```

45. A Woman's Beauty is Measured By

- ADORN
- APPAREL
- ARRAY
- BEAUTIFUL
- BEAUTY
- CLOTHES
- COMES
- DECENT
- DEVOTED
- EXPENSIVE
- FANCY
- FAVOUR
- FIX
- GENTLE
- GODLINESS
- GOLD
- HAIR
- HAIRSTYLES
- HOLY
- JEWELRY
- MANNER
- MODEST
- OUTWARD
- PEARLS
- PRECIOUS
- QUIET
- SOBRIETY
- SPIRIT
- VAIN
- WITHIN

46. Afflicted Daughters of Abraham

Luke 13:11-16

And, behold, there was a woman which had a spirit of <u>infirmity</u> <u>eighteen</u> years, and was <u>bowed</u> together, and could in no wise <u>lift</u> up *herself*. And when Jesus saw her, he called *her to him*, and said unto her, Woman, thou <u>art</u> <u>loosed</u> from <u>thine</u> infirmity. And he laid *his* hands on her: and immediately she was made <u>straight</u>, and <u>glorified</u> God. And the ruler of the synagogue answered with <u>indignation</u>, because that Jesus had healed on the <u>sabbath</u> day, and said unto the people, There are <u>six</u> days in which men ought to work: in them therefore come and be <u>healed</u>, and not on the sabbath day. The Lord then answered him, and said, *Thou* <u>hypocrite</u>, doth not each one of you on the sabbath loose his <u>ox</u> or *his* ass from the <u>stall</u>, and lead *him* away to <u>watering</u>? And ought not this woman, being a daughter of <u>Abraham</u>, whom Satan hath bound, lo, these eighteen years, be loosed from this <u>bond</u> on the sabbath day? (KJV)

and a woman was there who had been <u>crippled</u> by a <u>spirit</u> for eighteen years. She was bent over and could not straighten up at all. When Jesus saw her, he called her forward and said to her, "Woman, you are set free from your infirmity." Then he put his hands on her, and immediately she straightened up and <u>praised</u> God.

Indignant because Jesus had healed on the Sabbath, the <u>synagogue</u> <u>ruler</u> said to the people, "There are six days for work. So come and be healed on those days, not on the Sabbath."

The Lord answered him, "You hypocrites! Doesn't each of you on the Sabbath <u>untie</u> his ox or <u>donkey</u> from the stall and lead it out to give it water? Then should not this woman, a <u>daughter</u> of Abraham, whom <u>Satan</u> has kept bound for eighteen long years, be set <u>free</u> on the Sabbath day from what <u>bound</u> her?" (NIV)

Bible Word Search, Vol. II: Women in the Bible

46. Afflicted Daughters of Abraham

ABRAHAM	GLORIFIED	SABBATH
ART	HEALED	SATAN
BOND	HYPOCRITE	SIX
BOUND	INDIGNATION	SPIRIT
BOWED	INFIRMITY	STALL
CRIPPLED	LIFT	STRAIGHT
DAUGHTER	LOOSED	SYNAGOGUE
DONKEY	OX	THINE
EIGHTEEN	PRAISED	UNTIE
FREE	RULER	WATER

47. Anna, The Prophetess

Luke 2:36-38

And there was one <u>Anna</u>, a <u>prophetess</u>, the daughter of <u>Phanuel</u>, of the <u>tribe</u> of Aser: she was of a <u>great</u> age, and had lived with an husband seven years from her virginity; And she *was* a <u>widow</u> of about <u>fourscore</u> and four years, which departed not from the <u>temple</u>, but served *God* with <u>fastings</u> and prayers night and day. And she coming in that <u>instant</u> gave thanks <u>likewise</u> unto the Lord, and spake of him to all them that looked for <u>redemption</u> in Jerusalem. (KJV)

There was also a prophetess, Anna, the daughter of Phanuel, of the tribe of <u>Asher</u>. She was very <u>old</u>; she had lived with her husband seven years after her marriage, and then was a widow <u>until</u> she was <u>eighty</u>-four. She never left the temple but <u>worshiped</u> night and day, fasting and praying. Coming up to them at that very <u>moment</u>, she gave <u>thanks</u> to God and spoke about the child to all who were looking <u>forward</u> to the redemption of <u>Jerusalem</u>. (NIV)

Anna, a prophet, was also there in the Temple. She was the daughter of Phanuel, of the tribe of Asher, and was very old. She was a widow, for her husband had <u>died</u> when they had been married only seven years. She was now eighty-four years old. She never left the Temple but <u>stayed</u> there day and <u>night</u>, worshiping God with fasting and prayer. She came along just as <u>Simeon</u> was <u>talking</u> with Mary and Joseph, and she began <u>praising</u> God. She talked about Jesus to everyone who had been <u>waiting</u> for the <u>promised</u> King to come and <u>deliver</u> Jerusalem. (NLT)

Bible Word Search, Vol. II: Women in the Bible

47. Anna, The Prophetess

ANNA	JERUSALEM	SIMEON
ASHER	LIKEWISE	STAYED
DELIVER	MOMENT	TALKING
DIED	NIGHT	TEMPLE
EIGHTY	OLD	THANKS
FASTINGS	PHANUEL	TRIBE
FORWARD	PRAISING	UNTIL
FOURSCORE	PROMISED	WAITING
GREAT	PROPHETESS	WIDOW
INSTANT	REDEMPTION	WORSHIPED

48. Daughters of Jerusalem

Luke 13:11-16

And as they led him away, they laid hold upon one <u>Simon</u>, a <u>Cyrenian</u>, coming out of the country, and on him they laid the cross, that he might <u>bear</u> *it* after Jesus. And there followed him a <u>great</u> company of people, and of women, which also <u>bewailed</u> and <u>lamented</u> him. But Jesus turning unto them said, Daughters of Jerusalem, <u>weep</u> not for me, but weep for yourselves, and for your children. For, behold, the days are coming, in the which they shall say, Blessed *are* the <u>barren</u>, and the <u>wombs</u> that never <u>bare</u>, and the <u>paps</u> which never gave <u>suck</u>. Then shall they begin to say to the mountains, Fall on us; and to the hills, <u>Cover</u> us… (KJV)

As they led him away, they <u>seized</u> Simon from Cyrene, who was on his way in from the country, and put the cross on him and made him <u>carry</u> it behind Jesus. A large number of people followed him, including women who <u>mourned</u> and wailed for him. Jesus turned and said to them, "Daughters of Jerusalem, do not weep for me; weep for yourselves and for your children. For the <u>time</u> will come when you will say, 'Blessed are the barren women, the wombs that never <u>bore</u> and the breasts that never <u>nursed</u>!' Then
"'they will say to the <u>mountains</u>, "Fall on us!"
and to the <u>hills</u>, "Cover us!"'"

As they led Jesus away, Simon of Cyrene, who was coming in from the <u>country</u> just then, was <u>forced</u> to follow Jesus and carry his <u>cross</u>. Great crowds <u>trailed</u> along behind, including many grief-<u>stricken</u> women. But Jesus turned and said to them, "Daughters of Jerusalem, don't weep for me, but weep for yourselves and for your children. For the days are coming when they will say, '<u>Fortunate</u> indeed are the women who are <u>childless</u>, the wombs that have not borne a child and the <u>breasts</u> that have never nursed.' (NLT)

Bible Word Search, Vol. II: Women in the Bible

48. Daughters of Jerusalem

- BARE
- BARREN
- BEAR
- BEWAILED
- BORE
- BREAST
- CARRY
- CHILDLESS
- COUNTRY
- COVER
- CROSS
- CYRENIAN
- FORCED
- FORTUNATE
- GREAT
- GRIEF
- HILLS
- LAMENTED
- MOUNTAINS
- MOURNED
- NURSED
- PAPS
- SEIZED
- SIMON
- STRICKEN
- SUCK
- TIME
- TRAILED
- WEEP
- WOMBS

49. Demon Possessed Damsel

And it came to pass, as we went to prayer, a certain <u>damsel</u> <u>possessed</u> with a spirit of <u>divination</u> met us, which <u>brought</u> her masters much gain by <u>soothsaying</u> (fortune-<u>teller</u>, NLT): The same followed <u>Paul</u> and us, and cried, saying, These men are the <u>servants</u> of the most high God, which show unto us the way of salvation. And this did she many days. But Paul, being <u>grieved</u>, <u>turned</u> and said to the spirit, I command thee in the name of Jesus Christ to come out of her. And he came out the same hour. And when her masters saw that the <u>hope</u> of their <u>gains</u> was gone, they caught Paul and <u>Silas</u>, and drew *them* into the <u>marketplace</u> unto the rulers, And brought them to the <u>magistrates</u>, saying, These men, being Jews, do exceedingly trouble our city, And teach <u>customs</u>, which are not <u>lawful</u> for us to receive, neither to <u>observe</u>, being Romans. And the multitude <u>rose</u> up together against them: and the magistrates rent off their clothes, and commanded to beat *them*. (<u>stripped</u> and <u>beaten</u> with wooden <u>rods</u>, NLT); And when they had laid many stripes upon them (severely flogged, NIV), they cast *them* into prison, charging the jailor to keep them safely: Who, having received such a charge, thrust them into the inner prison, and made their feet fast in the <u>stocks</u>.

And at <u>midnight</u> Paul and Silas prayed, and sang praises unto God: and the prisoners heard them. And suddenly there was a great earthquake, so that the <u>foundations</u> of the <u>prison</u> were <u>shaken</u>: and immediately all the doors were opened, and every one's bands were loosed. And the keeper of the prison awaking out of his sleep, and seeing the prison doors open, he drew out his sword, and would have killed himself, supposing that the prisoners had been fled. But Paul cried with a loud voice, saying, Do thyself no harm: for we are all here. Then he called for a light, and <u>sprang</u> in, and came <u>trembling</u>, and fell down before Paul and Silas, And brought them out ... (Acts 16:16-30 KJV)

Bible Word Search, Vol. II: Women in the Bible

49. Demon-Possessed Damsel

BEATEN	LAWFUL	SERVANTS
BROUGHT	MAGISTRATES	SHAKEN
CUSTOMS	MARKETPLACE	SILAS
DAMSEL	MIDNIGHT	SOOTHSAYING
DIVINATION	OBSERVE	SPRANG
FORTUNE	PAUL	STOCKS
FOUNDATIONS	POSSESSED	STRIPPED
GAINS	PRISON	TELLER
GRIEVED	RODS	TREMBLING
HOPE	ROSE	TURNED

50. Dorcas (Tabitha)

There was a <u>believer</u> in <u>Joppa</u> named <u>Tabitha</u> (which in Greek is <u>Dorcas</u>). She was always doing <u>kind</u> things for others and <u>helping</u> the poor. About this time she became <u>ill</u> and died. Her <u>friends</u> prepared her for <u>burial</u> and <u>laid</u> her in an <u>upstairs</u> room. But they had <u>heard</u> that <u>Peter</u> was <u>nearby</u> at <u>Lydda</u>, so they sent two men to beg him, "Please come as soon as possible!"

So Peter returned with them; and as soon as he <u>arrived</u>, they took him to the upstairs room. The room was filled with widows who were <u>weeping</u> and showing him the <u>coats</u> and other <u>garments</u> Dorcas had made for them. But Peter asked them all to leave the room; then he <u>knelt</u> and prayed. Turning to the body he said, "Get up, Tabitha." And she opened her eyes! When she <u>saw</u> Peter, she sat up! He gave her his <u>hand</u> and helped her up. Then he called in the widows and all the believers, and he <u>showed</u> them that she was <u>alive</u>.

The news <u>raced</u> through the <u>whole</u> <u>town</u>, and many believed in the Lord. And Peter stayed a long time in Joppa, living with <u>Simon</u>, a <u>leather-worker</u>. (Acts 9:36-43 NLT)

Bible Word Search, Vol. II: Women in the Bible

```
A D O R C A S T A B I T H A D
L E A T H E R R Q G W D E V D
I W P E T E R V P J J G L W O
V O H W I I G H F R A P P O J
E H A E V L R R R S R P I R X
G S N E A R B Y S T L E N K B
X Y D P S R A S O A L J G E F
J Q N I O R D W H O L E L R G
G N M N O V N E G C O I I E A
T O L G J S A W F C E E L R R
N L A I D I L I Y V N H Q L M
H H I D L R A C E D L D Y P E
G S R D Y I S R S D N D V A N
C Y U P S T A I R S D I Q X T
U P B F Y E K T G A F M K D S
```

COPYRIGHT © GIL PUBLICATIONS 2006

50. Dorcas (Tabitha)

ALIVE	HELPING	RACED
ARRIVED	ILL	SAW
BELIEVER	JOPPA	SHOWED
BURIAL	KIND	SIMON
COATS	KNELT	TABITHA
DORCAS	LAID	TOWN
FRIENDS	LEATHER	UPSTAIRS
GARMENTS	LYDDA	WEEPING
HAND	NEARBY	WHOLE
HEARD	PETER	WORKER

51. Elizabeth

It all begins with a Jewish priest, Zechariah, who lived when Herod was king of Judea. Zechariah was a member of the priestly order of Abijah. His wife, Elizabeth, was also from the priestly line of Aaron. Zechariah and Elizabeth were righteous in God's eyes, careful to obey all of the Lord's commandments and regulations. They had no children because Elizabeth was barren, and now they were both very old ...
But the angel said, "Don't be afraid, Zechariah! For God has heard your prayer, and your wife, Elizabeth, will bear you a son! And you are to name him John ...
Soon afterward his wife, Elizabeth, became pregnant and went into seclusion for five months ...
In the sixth month of Elizabeth's pregnancy, God sent the angel Gabriel to Nazareth, a village in Galilee ...(to Mary)
What's more, your relative Elizabeth has become pregnant in her old age! People used to say she was barren, but she's already in her sixth month ...
A few days later Mary hurried to the hill country of Judea, to the town where Zechariah lived. She entered the house and greeted Elizabeth. At the sound of Mary's greeting, Elizabeth's child leaped within her, and Elizabeth was filled with the Holy Spirit...
Elizabeth gave a glad cry and exclaimed to Mary, "You are blessed by God above all other women, and your child is blessed. ...
Mary stayed with Elizabeth about three months and then went back to her own home ...
Now it was time for Elizabeth's baby to be born, and it was a boy. When the baby was eight days old, all the relatives and friends came for the circumcision ceremony. They wanted to name him Zechariah, after his father.
But Elizabeth said, "No! His name is John!" ... (Luke 1 NLT)

Bible Word Search, Vol. II: Women in the Bible

```
R B O R O M N A Z A R E T H
E D L I H C B H A J I B A A
L O W N C E R E M O N Y A D
A S B N L U F E R A C E R N
T U L R X O R D E R D A H D
I O E O N O R A A U E O L Y
V E S B M A R Y J H J O M V
E T S I H O L Y S P I R I T
S H E N O S R L N E B A G T
X G D N A M E E E I E G P
H I K R E H T O Y A R G A E
X R L E I R B A G A P R H R
I E L I Z A B E T H R E A T
Q X N O I S U L C E S P D B
```

COPYRIGHT © GIL PUBLICATIONS 2006

51. Elizabeth

AARON	EIGHT	NAZARETH
ABIJAH	ELIZABETH	OLD
AGE	GABRIEL	ORDER
BARREN	HEARD	OTHER
BEAR	HOLYSPIRIT	OWN
BLESSED	JOHN	PRAYER
BORN	JUDEA	RELATIVES
CAREFUL	LEAPED	RIGHTEOUS
CEREMONY	MARY	SECLUSION
CHILD	NAME	SON

GIL Publications, P. O. Box 80275, Brooklyn, NY 11208
www.BibleWordSearchPuzzles.com

52. Euodia and Syntyche

Philippians 4:1-3

Therefore, my beloved <u>brethren</u> whom I long *to see*, my <u>joy</u> and <u>crown</u>, in this way <u>stand</u> <u>firm</u> in the Lord, my beloved.
I urge <u>Euodia</u> and I <u>urge</u> <u>Syntyche</u> to live in <u>harmony</u> in the Lord. Indeed, true <u>companion</u>, I ask you also to help these women who have shared my struggle in *the cause of* the <u>gospel</u>, <u>together</u> with <u>Clement</u> also and the rest of my fellow workers, whose names are in the book of life. (NASB)

Therefore, my brethren <u>dearly</u> beloved and longed for, my joy and crown, so stand <u>fast</u> in the Lord, *my* dearly beloved. I beseech Euodias, and <u>beseech</u> Syntyche, that they be of the <u>same</u> mind in the Lord. And I entreat thee also, true <u>yokefellow</u>, help those women which <u>laboured</u> with me in the gospel, with Clement also, and *with* other my <u>fellowlabourers</u>, whose names *are* in the book of life. (KJV)

Therefore, my brothers, you whom I love and long for, my joy and crown, that is how you should stand firm in the Lord, dear <u>friends</u>!
I plead with Euodia and I <u>plead</u> with Syntyche to <u>agree</u> with each other in the Lord. ³Yes, and I ask you, loyal yokefellow, help these women who have <u>contended</u> at my side in the cause of the gospel, along with Clement and the rest of my fellow workers, whose names are in the book of life. (NIV)

Dear brothers and sisters, I love you and long to see you, for you are my joy and the reward for my work. So please stay true to the Lord, my dear friends.
And now I want to plead with those two women, Euodia and Syntyche. Please, because you belong to the Lord, <u>settle</u> your <u>disagreement</u>. And I ask you, my true teammate, to help these women, for they worked hard with me in <u>telling</u> others the <u>Good</u> <u>News</u>. And they worked with Clement and the <u>rest</u> of my co-workers, whose names are written in the Book of Life. (NLT)

Bible Word Search, Vol. II: Women in the Bible

52. Euodia and Syntyche

- AGREE
- BESEECH
- BRETHREN
- CLEMENT
- COMPANION
- CONTENDED
- CROWN
- DEARLY
- DISAGREEMENT
- EUODIA
- FAST
- FELLOWLABOURERS
- FIRM
- FRIENDS
- GOOD
- GOSPEL
- HARMONY
- JOY
- LABOURED
- NEWS
- PLEAD
- REST
- SAME
- SETTLE
- STAND
- SYNTYCHE
- TELLING
- TOGETHER
- URGE
- YOKEFELLOW

53. Godly Wives

Submit to one another out of <u>reverence</u> for Christ.

Wives, <u>submit</u> to your husbands as to the Lord. For the husband is the head of the <u>wife</u> as Christ is the head of the church, his <u>body</u>, of which he is the Savior. Now as the <u>church</u> submits to Christ, so also wives should submit to their husbands in everything.

Husbands, love your wives, just as Christ <u>loved</u> the church and gave himself up for her to make her <u>holy</u>, <u>cleansing</u> her by the <u>washing</u> with <u>water</u> through the word, and to present her to himself as a <u>radiant</u> church, without <u>stain</u> or <u>wrinkle</u> or any other <u>blemish</u>, but holy and <u>blameless</u>. In this same way, husbands ought to love their wives as their own bodies. He who loves his wife loves himself. After all, no one ever hated his <u>own</u> body, but he feeds and cares for it, just as <u>Christ</u> does the church—for we are <u>members</u> of his body. "For this reason a man will <u>leave</u> his father and mother and be <u>united</u> to his wife, and the two will become one <u>flesh</u>."This is a <u>profound</u> mystery—but I am talking about Christ and the church. However, each one of you also must love his wife as he loves himself, and the wife must <u>respect</u> her husband. (Ephesians 5:21-22 NIV)

To the <u>married</u> I give this command (not I, but the Lord): A wife must not <u>separate</u> from her husband. But if she does, she must <u>remain</u> unmarried or else be reconciled to her husband. And a husband must not divorce his wife.

To the rest I say this (I, not the Lord): If any brother has a wife who is not a believer and she is willing to <u>live</u> with him, he must not <u>divorce</u> her. And if a woman has a husband who is not a believer and he is willing to live with her, she must not divorce him. For the <u>unbelieving</u> husband has been sanctified through his wife, and the unbelieving wife has been sanctified through her believing <u>husband</u>. (1 Corinthians 7:10-14a NIV)

Bible Word Search, Vol. II: Women in the Bible

```
E R E T A W D S R E B M E M H
G E F Y A I E E G X L W L I B
N S L B L F V D N U O F O R P
I P E R H E O Y I W Y D G W S
V E S D R Y L O H S I M E L B
E C H E A V D Y S U B A L I A
I T N I D C L E A N S I N G K
L C H R I S T N W O P B O D Y
E H A R A P D N R R E M A I N
B U O A N E L Z I R H E D N Z
N R X M T X M G N A V T L X D
U C T I M B U S K I T B E U B
K H N B L A M E L E S S A G U
F U N Q F B R W E C R O V I D
W T O G P E E T A R A P E S U
```

COPYRIGHT © GIL PUBLICATIONS 2006

53. Godly Wives

BLAMELESS	LEAVE	REVERENCE
BLEMISH	LIVE	SEPARATE
BODY	LOVED	STAIN
CHRIST	MARRIED	SUBMIT
CHURCH	MEMBERS	UNBELIEVING
CLEANSING	OWN	UNITED
DIVORCE	PROFOUND	WASHING
FLESH	RADIANT	WATER
HOLY	REMAIN	WIFE
HUSBAND	RESPECT	WRINKLE

GIL Publications, P. O. Box 80275, Brooklyn, NY 11208
www.BibleWordSearchPuzzles.com

54. Herodias and the Beheading of John the Baptist

For <u>Herod</u> <u>himself</u> had sent forth and laid hold upon John, and <u>bound</u> him in <u>prison</u> for <u>Herodias'</u> <u>sake</u>, his <u>brother</u> Philip's wife: for he had married her.

For John had said unto Herod, It is not lawful for thee to have thy brother's wife.

Therefore Herodias had a <u>quarrel</u> against him, and would have <u>killed</u> him; but she could not:

For Herod <u>feared</u> John, knowing that he was a just man and an <u>holy</u>, and observed him; and when he heard him, he did many things, and heard him gladly.

And when a convenient day was come, that Herod on his birthday made a <u>supper</u> to his lords, high captains, and chief estates of <u>Galilee</u>;

And when the <u>daughter</u> of the said Herodias came in, and <u>danced</u>, and pleased Herod and them that sat with him, the king said unto the <u>damsel</u>, Ask of me whatsoever thou <u>wilt</u>, and I will give it thee.

And he sware unto her, Whatsoever thou shalt ask of me, I will give it thee, unto the half of my kingdom.

And she went <u>forth</u>, and said unto her mother, What shall I ask? And she said, The head of <u>John</u> the <u>Baptist</u>.

And she came in straightway with <u>haste</u> unto the king, and asked, saying, I will that thou give me by and by in a charger the head of John the Baptist.

And the king was <u>exceeding</u> <u>sorry</u>; yet for his <u>oath</u>'s sake, and for their sakes which sat with him, he would not reject her.

And immediately the king sent an <u>executioner</u>, and commanded his head to be brought: and he went and <u>beheaded</u> him in the prison,

And brought his head in a charger, and gave it to the damsel: and the damsel gave it to her mother.

And when his <u>disciples</u> heard of it, they came and <u>took</u> up his <u>corpse</u>, and laid it in a <u>tomb</u>. (Mark 6:17-29 KJV)

Bible Word Search, Vol. II: Women in the Bible

```
T L I W S A I D O R E H G C V
B R O T H E R A Z E J L O B L
E F O R T H L K T C T O C L A
X D O A T H Z E K A S S H T Y
C A T S I T P A B M K P A N R
E U Q U A R R E L G W R D H E
E G S S U P P E R A B I Q X N
D H E B H E R O D L O S E E O
I T L M Q O C Y Z I U O H E I
N E P O D O R L E L N N I L T
G R I T R R P R Z E D T M E U
K W C P O D A N C E D E S S C
O S S S U F E A R E D D E M E
O E I K U K I L L E D C L A X
T B D B E H E A D E D C F D E
```

COPYRIGHT © GIL PUBLICATIONS 2006

54. Herodias & the Beheading of John the Baptist

BAPTIST	EXECUTIONER	KILLED
BEHEADED	FEARED	OATH
BOUND	FORTH	PRISON
BROTHER	GALILEE	QUARREL
CORPSE	HASTE	SAKE
DAMSEL	HEROD	SORRY
DANCED	HERODIAS	SUPPER
DAUGHTER	HIMSELF	TOMB
DISCIPLES	HOLY	TOOK
EXCEEDING	JOHN	WILT

GIL Publications, P. O. Box 80275, Brooklyn, NY 11208
www.BibleWordSearchPuzzles.com

55. Jairus' Daughter

As Jesus was saying this, the leader of a synagogue came and <u>knelt</u> down before him. "My daughter has just <u>died</u>," he said, "but you can <u>bring</u> her back to <u>life</u> <u>again</u> if you just come and lay your hand upon her." As Jesus and the disciples were going to the <u>official</u>'s <u>home</u>, (Matthew 9:18-19 NLT)

When Jesus entered the ruler's <u>house</u> and saw the flute players and the <u>noisy</u> crowd, he said, "Go away. The girl is not dead but <u>asleep</u>." But they <u>laughed</u> at him. After the crowd had been put outside, he went in and took the girl by the hand, and she got up. News of this <u>spread</u> through all that <u>region</u>. (Matthew 9:23-25 NIV)

And when Jesus was passed over again by <u>ship</u> unto the other side, much people <u>gathered</u> unto him: and he was <u>nigh</u> unto the sea. And, behold, there cometh one of the rulers of the synagogue, <u>Jairus</u> by name; and when he saw him, he fell at his feet, And besought him greatly, saying, My little daughter <u>lieth</u> at the <u>point</u> of death: *I pray thee*, come and lay thy hands on her, that she may be healed; and she shall live. And *Jesus* went with him; and much people followed him, and <u>thronged</u> him. (Mark 5:21-24 KJV)

While he was still speaking to her, <u>messengers</u> arrived from Jairus's home with the message, "Your daughter is dead. There's no use <u>troubling</u> the Teacher now."

But Jesus <u>ignored</u> their comments and said to Jairus, "Don't be afraid. Just trust me." Then Jesus stopped the crowd and wouldn't let anyone go with him <u>except</u> Peter and James and John. When they came to the home of the synagogue leader, Jesus saw the <u>commotion</u> and the weeping and wailing. He went inside and spoke to the people. "Why all this <u>weeping</u> and commotion?" he asked. "The child isn't dead; she is only asleep."

The crowd laughed at him, but he told them all to go outside. Then he took the girl's father and mother and his three disciples into the room where the girl was <u>lying</u>. <u>Holding</u> her hand, he said to her, "Get up, little girl!" And the girl, who was twelve years old, immediately stood up and walked around! Her parents were <u>absolutely</u> <u>overwhelmed</u>. (Mark 5:35-42 NLT)

Bible Word Search, Vol. II: Women in the Bible

55. Jairus' Daughter

ABSOLUTELY	HOUSE	NOISY
AGAIN	IGNORED	OFFICIAL
ASLEEP	JAIRUS	OVERWHELMED
BRING	KNELT	POINT
COMMOTION	LAUGHED	REGION
DIED	LIETH	SHIP
EXCEPT	LIFE	SPREAD
GATHERED	LYING	THRONGED
HOLDING	MESSENGERS	TROUBLING
HOME	NIGH	WEEPING

GIL Publications, P. O. Box 80275, Brooklyn, NY 11208
www.BibleWordSearchPuzzles.com

56. Jesus' Sisters

Jesus left there and went to his <u>hometown</u>, <u>accompanied</u> by his disciples. When the Sabbath came, he began to <u>teach</u> in the <u>synagogue</u>, and many who <u>heard</u> him were <u>amazed</u>.

"Where did this man get these things?" they asked. "What's this wisdom that has been given him, that he even does <u>miracles</u>! <u>Isn't</u> this the <u>carpenter</u>? Isn't this Mary's son and the brother of <u>James</u>, <u>Joseph</u>, <u>Judas</u> and <u>Simon</u>? Aren't his sisters here with us?" And they took <u>offense</u> at him.

Jesus said to them, "Only in his hometown, among his <u>relatives</u> and in his own house is a prophet without honor." He could not do any miracles there, except <u>lay</u> his hands on a <u>few</u> <u>sick</u> people and <u>heal</u> them. And he was amazed at their <u>lack</u> of <u>faith</u>. (Mark 6:1-6 NIV)

When Jesus had finished telling these stories, he left that part of the country. He returned to <u>Nazareth</u>, his hometown. When he taught there in the synagogue, everyone was <u>astonished</u> and said, "Where does he get his <u>wisdom</u> and his miracles? He's just a carpenter's son, and we know Mary, his mother, and his brothers—James, Joseph, Simon, and Judas. All his sisters live right here among us. What makes him so great?" And they were deeply <u>offended</u> and <u>refused</u> to believe in him.

Then Jesus told them, "A <u>prophet</u> is <u>honored</u> everywhere <u>except</u> in his own hometown and among his own <u>family</u>." And so he did only a few miracles there because of their unbelief. (Matthew 13:55-56 NLT)

Bible Word Search, Vol. II: Women in the Bible

```
K Z H H F E W A T E H P O R P
H C A E T X I M I R A C L E S
E H A A J O S E P H G M R T E
A T T L S A D U J A M E S N V
R K C I S H O N O R E D Y E I
D E I N A P M O C C A N L P T
X E S N E F F O Z R R A I R A
W H H O M E T O W N Y R M A L
U N Y S Y N A G O G U E A C E
H G U X I S N T D E S U F E R
O P W D E N A Z A R E T H R D
Y O V H X Z O F F E N D E D E
Z A Q O X N B T P E C X E Z W
S U E R U Z Q A S I M O N S C
W U Z I Y Q U Z U A M A Z E D
```

COPYRIGHT © GIL PUBLICATIONS 2006

56. Jesus' Sisters

ACCOMPANIED	HOMETOWN	OFFENDED
AMAZED	HONORED	OFFENSE
ASTONISHED	ISNT	PROPHET
CARPENTER	JAMES	REFUSED
EXCEPT	JOSEPH	RELATIVES
FAITH	JUDAS	SICK
FAMILY	LACK	SIMON
FEW	LAY	SYNAGOGUE
HEAL	MIRACLES	TEACH
HEARD	NAZARETH	WISDOM

GIL Publications, P. O. Box 80275, Brooklyn, NY 11208
www.BibleWordSearchPuzzles.com

57. Lydia

Acts 16:14-15, 40

And a certain woman named <u>Lydia</u>, a <u>seller</u> of <u>purple</u>, of the city of <u>Thyatira</u>, which <u>worshipped</u> God, heard *us*: whose heart the Lord opened, that she <u>attended</u> unto the things which were spoken of <u>Paul</u>. And when she was <u>baptized</u>, and her household, she <u>besought</u> *us*, saying, If ye have judged me to be <u>faithful</u> to the Lord, come into my house, and <u>abide</u> *there*. And she <u>constrained</u> us.

... And they went out of the prison, and entered into *the house of Lydia*: and when they had seen the <u>brethren</u>, they <u>comforted</u> them, and departed. (KJV)

One of those <u>listening</u> was a woman named Lydia, a <u>dealer</u> in purple cloth from the <u>city</u> of Thyatira, who was a worshiper of God. The Lord opened her heart to respond to Paul's <u>message</u>. When she and the <u>members</u> of her household were baptized, she invited us to her home. "If you consider me a believer in the Lord," she said, "come and stay at my house." And she <u>persuaded</u> us.

... After Paul and Silas came out of the <u>prison</u>, they went to Lydia's house, where they met with the brothers and <u>encouraged</u> them. Then they left. (NIV)

One of them was Lydia from Thyatira, a <u>merchant</u> of <u>expensive</u> purple <u>cloth</u>. She was a worshiper of God. As she listened to us, the Lord opened her heart, and she <u>accepted</u> what Paul was saying. She was baptized along with other members of her household, and she asked us to be her <u>guests</u>. "If you agree that I am faithful to the Lord," she said, "come and stay at my home." And she <u>urged</u> us until we did.

... Paul and <u>Silas</u> then returned to the home of Lydia, where they met with the believers and encouraged them once more before <u>leaving</u> town. (NLT)

Bible Word Search, Vol. II: Women in the Bible

```
K N E R H T E R B A B I D E W
C O P A C T H G U O S E B T H
O S E C L D E Z I T P A B N O
N I R C O B K B L P A U L A K
S R S E T J H Y I C H E W H G
T P U P H C D H S I L A S C N
R S A T Y I S G U E S T S R I
A R D E A R I T A Y H T S E N
I E E D O U E G A S S E M M E
N B D W N D L E A V I N G P T
E M E X P E N S I V E D X U S
D E A L E R U O U R G E D R I
M M E N C O U R A G E D N P L
N C I T Y V F A I T H F U L A
D E T R O F M O C R E L L E S
```

COPYRIGHT © GIL PUBLICATIONS 2006

57. Lydia

ABIDE	DEALER	MESSAGE
ACCEPTED	ENCOURAGED	PAUL
ATTENDED	EXPENSIVE	PERSUADED
BAPTIZED	FAITHFUL	PRISON
BESOUGHT	GUESTS	PURPLE
BRETHREN	LEAVING	SELLER
CITY	LISTENING	SILAS
CLOTH	LYDIA	THYATIRA
COMFORTED	MEMBERS	URGED
CONSTRAINED	MERCHANT	WORSHIPPED

GIL Publications, P. O. Box 80275, Brooklyn, NY 11208
www.BibleWordSearchPuzzles.com

58. Mary and Martha with Lazarus

When <u>Martha</u> heard that Jesus was coming, she <u>went</u> out to <u>meet</u> him, but <u>Mary</u> <u>stayed</u> at home.

"Lord," Martha said to Jesus, "if you had been here, my <u>brother</u> would not have <u>died</u>. [22]But I know that even now God will give you whatever you ask."

Jesus said to her, "Your brother will <u>rise</u> again."

Martha answered, "I know he will rise again in the resurrection at the last day."

Jesus said to her, "I am the resurrection and the life. He who believes in me will live, even though he dies; [26]and whoever lives and believes in me will never die. Do you believe this?"

"Yes, Lord," she told him, "I believe that you are the Christ,[2] the Son of God, who was to come into the world."

And after she had said this, she went back and called her <u>sister</u> Mary aside. "The <u>Teacher</u> is here," she said, "and is <u>asking</u> for you." When Mary heard this, she got up <u>quickly</u> and went to him. Now Jesus had not yet entered the <u>village</u>, but was still at the <u>place</u> where Martha had met him. When the Jews who had been with Mary in the <u>house</u>, <u>comforting</u> her, noticed how quickly she got up and went out, they followed her, supposing she was going to the <u>tomb</u> to <u>mourn</u> there.

When Mary reached the place where Jesus was and saw him, she fell at his feet and said, "Lord, if you had been here, my brother would not have died." When Jesus saw her weeping, and the Jews who had come along with her also weeping, he was <u>deeply</u> <u>moved</u> in spirit and <u>troubled</u>. "Where have you laid him?" he asked.

"Come and see, Lord," they replied.

Jesus <u>wept</u>.

Then the Jews said, "See how he loved him!"

But some of them said, "Could not he who opened the <u>eyes</u> of the blind man have kept this man from dying?"

Jesus, once more deeply moved, came to the tomb. It was a <u>cave</u> with a <u>stone</u> laid across the entrance. [39]"Take away the stone," he said.

"But, Lord," said Martha, the sister of the <u>dead</u> man, "by this time there is a <u>bad</u> <u>odor</u>, for he has been there <u>four</u> days." (John 11:20-39 NIV)

Bible Word Search, Vol. II: Women in the Bible

```
K R E T S I S D B E D Q R A L
G H Q P Q X I T S E Q I M S A
E N X E T E R U V R S E A K C
P E I W D O O O U E Q N R I F
D S Q T U H M O C A V E T N R
E B M B R C F N R U O M H G R
J Z L D E O E C A L P R A C E
A E A N O W F E G A L L I V H
D Y O T E E P M M A R Y R L C
S T E N R O D O O S L I Z O A
S E T S T A Y E D C E S E M E
M D E E P L Y G N E B W E F T
X Z Y S H F F V A M F B S Y Q
Q U I C K L Y U O D A U N J E
B R O T H E R T E D D A E D F
```

COPYRIGHT © GIL PUBLICATIONS 2006

58. Mary, Martha and Lazarus

ASKING	FOUR	RISE
BAD	HOUSE	SISTER
BROTHER	MARTHA	STAYED
CAVE	MARY	STONE
COMFORTING	MEET	TEACHER
DAYS	MOURN	TOMB
DEAD	MOVED	TROUBLED
DEEPLY	ODOR	VILLAGE
DIED	PLACE	WENT
EYES	QUICKLY	WEPT

GIL Publications, P. O. Box 80275, Brooklyn, NY 11208
www.BibleWordSearchPuzzles.com

59. Mary and Martha: Only One Thing Is Needed

As Jesus and the disciples continued on their way to Jerusalem, they came to a village where a woman named Martha <u>welcomed</u> them into her <u>home</u>.

Her sister, <u>Mary</u>, <u>sat</u> at the Lord's feet, <u>listening</u> to what he <u>taught</u>.

But Martha was <u>worrying</u> over the <u>big</u> <u>dinner</u> she was <u>preparing</u>. She came to Jesus and said, "Lord, doesn't it <u>seem</u> <u>unfair</u> to you that my sister <u>just</u> <u>sits</u> here while I do all the <u>work</u>? <u>Tell</u> her to come and <u>help</u> <u>me</u>."

But the Lord said to her, "My <u>dear</u> <u>Martha</u>, you are so <u>upset</u> over all <u>these</u> <u>details</u>!

There is really <u>only</u> <u>one</u> thing <u>worth</u> <u>being</u> <u>concerned</u> <u>about</u>. Mary has <u>discovered</u> it--and I won't take it away from her." (Luke 10:38-42 NLT)

Bible Word Search, Vol. II: Women in the Bible

```
O T M A R T H A X L L E T M T
P N H G O Z W R M T A S A E D
R W L E Y F O E D N T R S E S
E E D Y S Q R N Z F Y P A M E
P L E B Q E T N C K U R J L E
A C T I Q G H I J U S T U U M
R O A G Z Y E D L U N F A I R
I M I D I S C O V E R E D E E
N E L G X J D E N R E C N O C
G D S B H Q T A U G H T J F G
A A G R E K M E L Y U E Q N W
S B P N L G N I N E T S I L U
S M O S P S O U Q F O E M O H
X F S U N O W O R K B M M Y E
S I T S T U G N I Y R R O W M
```

Copyright © GIL Publications 2006

59. Mary and Martha: Only One Thing Is Needed

ABOUT	JUST	SITS
BEING	LISTENING	TAUGHT
BIG	MARTHA	TELL
CONCERNED	MARY	THESE
DEAR	ME	UNFAIR
DETAILS	ONE	UPSET
DINNER	ONLY	WELCOMED
DISCOVERED	PREPARING	WORK
HELP	SAT	WORRYING
HOME	SEEM	WORTH

GIL Publications, P. O. Box 80275, Brooklyn, NY 11208
www.BibleWordSearchPuzzles.com

60. Mary Anoints Jesus, Woman with Alabaster Box

It was ... Mary which <u>anointed</u> the Lord with ointment, and <u>wiped</u> his feet with her <u>hair</u>. (John 11:2 KJV)

There came unto him a woman having an <u>alabaster</u> <u>box</u> of very precious <u>ointment</u>, and <u>poured</u> it on his head, as he sat at <u>meat</u>.

But when his disciples saw it, they had indignation, saying, To what <u>purpose</u> is this <u>waste</u>? For this ointment might have been <u>sold</u> for <u>much</u>, and <u>given</u> to the <u>poor</u>.

When Jesus <u>understood</u> it, he said unto them, Why trouble ye the woman? for she hath wrought a <u>good</u> work upon me. For ye have the poor always with you; but me ye have not always.

For in that she hath poured this ointment on my body, she did it for my burial. <u>Verily</u> I say unto you, Wheresoever this gospel shall be preached in the whole world, there shall also this, that this woman hath done, be told for a memorial of her. (Matthew 26: 7-13 KJV)

... a woman came to him with an alabaster <u>jar</u> of very <u>expensive</u> <u>perfume</u>, which she poured on his head as he was <u>reclining</u> at the <u>table</u>. When the disciples saw this, they were indignant. "Why this waste?" they asked. "This perfume could have been sold at a <u>high</u> <u>price</u> and the <u>money</u> given to the poor."

Aware of this, Jesus said to them, "Why are you bothering this woman? She has done a <u>beautiful</u> thing to me. The poor you will always have with you, but you will not always have me. When she poured this perfume on my body, she did it to <u>prepare</u> me for burial. I tell you the truth, wherever this gospel is preached throughout the world, what she has <u>done</u> will also be told, in <u>memory</u> of her." (Matthew 26: 7-13 NIV)

60. Mary Anoints Jesus

ALABASTER	JAR	PREPARE
ANOINTED	MEAT	PRICE
BEAUTIFUL	MEMORY	PURPOSE
BOX	MONEY	RECLINING
DONE	MUCH	SOLD
EXPENSIVE	OINTMENT	TABLE
GIVEN	PERFUME	UNDERSTOOD
GOOD	POOR	VERILY
HAIR	POURED	WASTE
HIGH	PRECIOUS	WIPED

61. Mary Magdalene

Her Deliverance
And it came to pass afterward, that he went throughout every city and village, preaching and shewing the glad tidings of the kingdom of God: and the twelve were with him, And certain women, which had been healed of evil spirits and infirmities, Mary called Magdalene, out of whom went seven devils ... (Luke 8:1-2 KJV)

At the Crucifixion and Burial of Jesus
And many women were there beholding afar off, which followed Jesus from Galilee, ministering unto him: Among which was Mary Magdalene ... (Matthew 27:55-56 KJV)

The First to See That Jesus Had Risen
The first day of the week cometh Mary Magdalene early, when it was yet dark, unto the sepulchre, and seeth the stone taken away from the sepulchre. Then she runneth, and cometh to Simon Peter, and to the other disciple, whom Jesus loved, and saith unto them, They have taken away the LORD out of the sepulchre, and we know not where they have laid him. Then the disciples went away again unto their own home. But Mary stood without at the sepulchre weeping: and as she wept, she stooped down, and looked into the sepulchre, And seeth two angels in white sitting, the one at the head, and the other at the feet, where the body of Jesus had lain. And they say unto her, Woman, why weepest thou? She saith unto them, Because they have taken away my LORD, and I know not where they have laid him.

And when she had thus said, she turned herself back, and saw Jesus standing, and knew not that it was Jesus.

Jesus saith unto her, Woman, why weepest thou? whom seekest thou? She, supposing him to be the gardener, saith unto him, Sir, if thou have borne him hence, tell me where thou hast laid him, and I will take him away.

Jesus saith unto her, Mary. She turned herself, and saith unto him, Rabboni; which is to say, Master.

Jesus saith unto her, Touch me not; for I am not yet ascended to my Father: but go to my brethren, and say unto them, I ascend unto my Father, and your Father; and to my God, and your God.

Mary Magdalene came and told the disciples that she had seen the LORD, and that he had spoken these things unto her. (John 20:2,11-18 KJV)

Bible Word Search, Vol. II: Women in the Bible

```
E P M K S D E W V V G S Z N G
R R I L A E W O E A A Y O N E
H A P L W B I J W W F T O T D
C B G X S E G T R T C M I K V
L B N R T H A H I Z A H B B Z
U O I F I O R T X M W E V I L
P N W Z R L D E P A R D A E H
E I E D I D E N D B N I O Y X
S T H T P I N N L O M G F T Q
S E S S S N E U S D X R E N O
O E S E A G R R T Y B Y A L I
K F V P Q T I D I N G S R F S
F N D E V I L S D N E C S A A
E F E E N S T A N D I N G S M
T V O W T P E N E L A D G A M
```

COPYRIGHT © GIL PUBLICATIONS 2006

61. Mary Magdalene

- AFAR
- AMONG
- ANGELS
- ASCEND
- BEHOLDING
- BODY
- DEVILS
- EVIL
- FEET
- GARDENER
- GLAD
- HEAD
- INFIRMITIES
- KNEW
- MAGDALENE
- MARY
- NOT
- OFF
- RABBONI
- RUNNETH
- SAW
- SEPULCHRE
- SEVEN
- SHEWING
- SPIRITS
- STANDING
- TIDINGS
- TWO
- WEEPEST
- WHITE

GIL Publications, P. O. Box 80275, Brooklyn, NY 11208
www.BibleWordSearchPuzzles.com

62. Mary, Mother of James and Joses

Then Jesus <u>uttered</u> another <u>loud</u> cry and <u>breathed</u> his last. And the <u>curtain</u> in the Temple was torn in two, from <u>top</u> to bottom. When the <u>Roman</u> <u>officer</u> who stood <u>facing</u> him saw how he had died, he <u>exclaimed</u>, "Truly, this was the Son of God!"

Some women were there, watching from a distance, including Mary Magdalene, Mary (the mother of James the younger and of Joseph), and Salome. They had been <u>followers</u> of Jesus and had cared for him while he was in Galilee. Then they and many other women had come with him to Jerusalem. (Mark 15:37-41 NLT)

Joseph took the body, <u>wrapped</u> it in a clean <u>linen</u> cloth, and placed it in his own new tomb that he had cut out of the <u>rock</u>. He rolled a big stone in front of the entrance to the tomb and went <u>away</u>. Mary Magdalene and the other Mary were sitting there <u>opposite</u> the tomb.

After the Sabbath, at <u>dawn</u> on the first day of the week, Mary Magdalene and the other Mary went to look at the tomb.

There was a violent <u>earthquake</u>, for an angel of the Lord came down from heaven and, going to the tomb, <u>rolled</u> back the stone and sat on it. His appearance was like <u>lightning</u>, and his clothes were <u>white</u> as snow. The guards were so afraid of him that they shook and became like dead men.

The angel said to the women, "Do not be afraid, for I know that you are looking for Jesus, who was <u>crucified</u>. He is not here; he has risen, just as he said. Come and see the place where he lay. Then go quickly and tell his disciples: 'He has <u>risen</u> from the dead and is going ahead of you into Galilee. There you will see him.' Now I have told you."

So the women <u>hurried</u> away from the tomb, <u>afraid</u> yet filled with joy, and ran to tell his disciples. Suddenly Jesus met them. "Greetings," he said. They came to him, <u>clasped</u> his feet and worshiped him. Then Jesus said to them, "Do not be afraid. Go and tell my <u>brothers</u> to go to Galilee; there they will see me." (Matthew 27:59-61; 28:1-10 NIV)

And returned from the sepulchre, and told all these things unto the eleven, and to all the rest. It was Mary Magdalene, and Joanna, and Mary *the mother* of James, and other *women that were* with them, which told these things unto the <u>apostles</u>. And their words seemed to them as idle <u>tales</u>, and they believed them not. Then arose Peter, and ran unto the sepulchre; and stooping down, he beheld the linen clothes laid by themselves, and departed, <u>wondering</u> in himself at that which was come to <u>pass</u>. (Luke 24:9-12 KJV)

Bible Word Search, Vol. II: Women in the Bible

```
B U T T E R E D Q O P L C V Y
C P A S S V T X O F F I C E R
S C L A S P E D E L L O R Y G
S R E W O L L O F H R O U G N
T U S E L T S O P A C Y C N I
I H U R R I E D W K A H I I A
V I H D E P P A R W P N F R T
E K A U Q H T R A E O F I E R
Z K D H L Q T V A O T S E D U
E T I S O P P O F O E I D N C
Z E L Q U U I I R N R H H O G
T J I E D L E K A B O D A W N
L G N I N T H G I L M W O P A
E X C L A I M E D F A C I N G
N B R E A T H E D D N E N I L
```

COPYRIGHT © GIL PUBLICATIONS 2006

62. Mary, Mother of James and Joses

AFRAID	EXCLAIMED	RISEN
APOSTLES	FACING	ROCK
AWAY	FOLLOWERS	ROLLED
BREATHED	HURRIED	ROMAN
BROTHERS	LIGHTNING	TALES
CLASPED	LINEN	TOP
CRUCIFIED	LOUD	UTTERED
CURTAIN	OFFICER	WHITE
DAWN	OPPOSITE	WONDERING
EARTHQUAKE	PASS	WRAPPED

GIL Publications, P. O. Box 80275, Brooklyn, NY 11208
www.BibleWordSearchPuzzles.com

63. Mary, Mother of Jesus

Now this is how Jesus the <u>Messiah</u> was <u>born</u>. His mother, Mary, was <u>engaged</u> to be married to Joseph. But while she was still a <u>virgin</u>, she became pregnant by the <u>Holy Spirit</u>. <u>Joseph</u>, her <u>fiance</u>, being a just man, decided to <u>break</u> the engagement quietly, so as not to <u>disgrace</u> her publicly.

As he considered this, he fell <u>asleep</u>, and an <u>angel</u> of the Lord appeared to him in a dream. "Joseph, son of David," the angel said, "do not be afraid to go <u>ahead</u> with your marriage to Mary. For the <u>child</u> within her has been conceived by the Holy Spirit. And she will have a <u>son</u>, and you are to name him Jesus, for he will save his <u>people</u> from their sins." All of this happened to fulfill the Lord's message through his prophet:

"Look! The virgin will conceive a child!

She will give birth to a son,

and he will be called <u>Immanuel</u> (meaning, God is with us)."

When Joseph <u>woke</u> up, he did what the angel of the Lord commanded. He brought Mary home to be his wife, but she remained a virgin until her son was born. And Joseph named him Jesus. (Matthew 1:18-25 NLT)

"Isn't this the <u>carpenter</u>'s son? Isn't his mother's name <u>Mary</u>, and aren't his brothers <u>James</u>, Joseph, <u>Simon</u> and <u>Judas</u>? Aren't all his <u>sisters</u> with us? (Matthew 13:55 NIV)

And suddenly there was with the angel a multitude of the heavenly host praising God, and saying, Glory to God in the <u>highest</u>, and on earth peace, good will toward men.

And it came to pass, as the angels were gone away from them into heaven, the <u>shepherds</u> said one to another, Let us now go even unto <u>Bethlehem</u>, and see this thing which is come to pass, which the Lord hath made known unto us.

And they came with haste, and found Mary, and Joseph, and the <u>babe</u> lying in a <u>manger</u> ...

But Mary kept all these things, and pondered them in her heart. (Luke 2:13-19 KJV)

Now there stood by the <u>cross</u> of Jesus his mother, and his mother's sister, Mary the wife of <u>Cleophas</u>, and Mary Magdalene. (John 19:25 KJV)

Bible Word Search, Vol. II: Women in the Bible

```
R T R N O S D I S G R A C E Y
X I Y R A M Q M I I F I N Z S
T R W O K E D M M E S S I A H
C I T B R Z W A O M X B G O E
H P Y M E E K N N B Z R R E P
M S F A S T C U B R B E I L H
W Y B N A A H E A D T A V P E
I L T G H H I L B N I K P O R
J O S E P H L C E N G A G E D
U H E R O Q D P F H F E V P S
D M H B E E R M N P E E L S A
A M G X L A Y V L J A M E S E
S X I E C N A I F Z D Q F O I
S E H B O L U I S I S T E R S
R L H T P C O C F C V Q F C Y
```

COPYRIGHT © GIL PUBLICATIONS 2006

63. Mary, Mother of Jesus

AHEAD	CROSS	MANGER
ANGEL	DISGRACE	MARY
ASLEEP	ENGAGED	MESSIAH
BABE	FIANCE	PEOPLE
BETHLEHEM	HIGHEST	SHEPHERDS
BORN	HOLYSPIRIT	SIMON
BREAK	IMMANUEL	SISTERS
CARPENTER	JAMES	SON
CHILD	JOSEPH	VIRGIN
CLEOPHAS	JUDAS	WOKE

GIL Publications, P. O. Box 80275, Brooklyn, NY 11208
www.BibleWordSearchPuzzles.com

64. Mary, Mother of Mark John, with Rhoda

Acts 12:11-16

And when Peter was come to himself, he said, Now I know of a <u>surety</u>, that the Lord hath sent his <u>angel</u>, and hath <u>delivered</u> me out of the hand of <u>Herod</u>, and *from* all the <u>expectation</u> of the people of the Jews. And when he had considered *the thing*, he came to the house of <u>Mary</u> the mother of <u>John</u>, whose <u>surname</u> was <u>Mark</u>; where many were <u>gathered</u> together praying. And as Peter <u>knocked</u> at the door of the <u>gate</u>, a <u>damsel</u> came to <u>hearken</u>, named Rhoda. And when she knew Peter's voice, she opened not the gate for <u>gladness</u>, but ran in, and told how Peter <u>stood</u> before the gate. And they said unto her, Thou art mad. But she constantly <u>affirmed</u> that it was even so. Then said they, It is his angel. But Peter continued knocking: and when they had opened *the door*, and saw him, they were <u>astonished</u>. (KJV)

Then Peter came to himself and said, "Now I know without a doubt that the Lord sent his angel and <u>rescued</u> me from Herod's <u>clutches</u> and from everything the Jewish people were <u>anticipating</u>."
When this had <u>dawned</u> on him, he went to the house of Mary the mother of John, also called Mark, where many people had gathered and were praying. <u>Peter</u> knocked at the outer entrance, and a servant girl named <u>Rhoda</u> came to <u>answer</u> the door. When she recognized Peter's voice, she was so <u>overjoyed</u> she ran back without opening it and exclaimed, "Peter is at the door!"
"You're out of your mind," they told her. When she kept insisting that it was so, they said, "It must be his angel." But Peter kept on knocking, and when they opened the door and saw him, they were astonished. (NIV)

Peter finally realized what had happened. "It's really true!" he said to himself. "The Lord has sent his angel and saved me from Herod and from what the Jews were <u>hoping</u> to do to me!"
After a little thought, he went to the home of Mary, the mother of John Mark, where many were gathered for prayer. He knocked at the door in the gate, and a servant girl named Rhoda came to open it. When she recognized Peter's <u>voice</u>, she was so overjoyed that, instead of opening the door, she ran back inside and told everyone, "Peter is standing at the door!"
"You're out of your mind," they said. When she insisted, they decided, "It must be his angel." <u>Meanwhile</u>, Peter continued knocking. When they finally went out and opened the door, they were <u>amazed</u>. (NLT)

Bible Word Search, Vol. II: Women in the Bible

```
D E U C S E R N S U R E T Y Q
N E H G A F F I R M E D B I C
N A Y B B T D E R E H T A G J
A S N O I T A T C E P X E N Y
D T S R J E H E A R K E N I D
N O E H B R C L P E T E R T A
W N H O J H E F S S R Y R A M
U I C D C G G V T M A R K P A
P S T A N C L H O P I N G I Z
G H U A B C F A O L V O I C E
D E L I V E R E D O R E H I D
W D C D E L I H W N A E M T Z
K N O C K E D A M S E L F N Y
A D A M N E D P R E W S N A T
R R H G A T E M A N R U S H P
```

COPYRIGHT © GIL PUBLICATIONS 2006

64. Mary, Mother of John Mark, with Rhoda

AFFIRMED	EXPECTATION	MARY
AMAZED	GATE	MEANWHILE
ANGEL	GATHERED	OVERJOYED
ANSWER	GLADNESS	PETER
ANTICIPATING	HEARKEN	RESCUED
ASTONISHED	HOPING	RHODA
CLUTCHES	HEROD	STOOD
DAMNED	JOHN	SURETY
DAMSEL	KNOCKED	SURNAME
DELIVERED	MARK	VOICE

GIL Publications, P. O. Box 80275, Brooklyn, NY 11208
www.BibleWordSearchPuzzles.com

65. Persistent Widow

Luke 18:1-8

And he spake a <u>parable</u> unto them *to this end*, that men ought always to pray, and not to <u>faint</u>; Saying, There was in a city a <u>judge</u>, which <u>feared</u> not God, neither regarded man:³And there was a widow in that city; and she came unto him, saying, <u>Avenge</u> me of mine <u>adversary</u>. And he would not for a while: but afterward he said within himself, Though I fear not God, nor regard man; Yet because this widow troubleth me, I will avenge her, lest by her continual coming she <u>weary</u> me. And the Lord said, Hear what the <u>unjust</u> judge saith. And shall not God avenge his own <u>elect</u>, which cry day and night unto him, though he bear long with them? I tell you that he will avenge them <u>speedily</u>. Nevertheless when the Son of man cometh, shall he find faith on the earth? (KJV)

One day Jesus told his disciples a story to <u>illustrate</u> their need for <u>constant</u> <u>prayer</u> and to show them that they must never give up. "There was a judge in a certain city," he said, "who was a <u>godless</u> man with great contempt for <u>everyone</u>. A widow of that city came to him repeatedly, <u>appealing</u> for justice against <u>someone</u> who had <u>harmed</u> her. The judge ignored her for a while, but <u>eventually</u> she wore him out. 'I fear neither God nor man,' he said to himself, 'but this woman is <u>driving</u> me <u>crazy</u>. I'm going to see that she gets <u>justice</u>, because she is wearing me out with her constant <u>requests</u>!'"

Then the Lord said, "Learn a lesson from this evil judge.⁷Even he <u>rendered</u> a just <u>decision</u> in the end, so don't you think God will surely give justice to his <u>chosen</u> people who <u>plead</u> with him day and night? Will he keep putting them off? I tell you, he will <u>grant</u> justice to them <u>quickly</u>! But when I, the Son of Man, <u>return</u>, how many will I find who have faith?" (NLT)

Bible Word Search, Vol. II: Women in the Bible

65. Persistent Widow

ADVERSARY	EVERYONE	PLEAD
APPEALING	FAINT	PRAYER
AVENGE	FEARED	QUICKLY
CHOSEN	GODLESS	RENDERED
CONSTANT	GRANT	REQUESTS
CRAZY	HARMED	RETURN
CRY	ILLUSTRATE	SOMEONE
DECISION	JUDGE	SPEEDILY
ELECT	JUSTICE	UNJUST
EVENTUALLY	PARABLE	WEARY

66. Peter's Mother-In-Law

Matthew 8:14-15

When Jesus came into Peter's house, he saw Peter's mother-in-law lying in bed with a fever. He touched her hand and the fever left her, and she got up and began to wait on him. (NIV)

And when Jesus was come into Peter's house, he saw his wife's mother laid, and sick of a fever.
And he touched her hand, and the fever left her: and she arose, and ministered unto them.(KJV)

And when Jesus went into Peter's house, He saw his mother-in-law lying ill with a fever.
He touched her hand and the fever left her; and she got up and began waiting on Him.(AMP)

When Jesus arrived at Peter's house, Peter's mother-in-law was in bed with a high fever. But when Jesus touched her hand, the fever left her. Then she got up and prepared a meal for him. (NLT)

Bible Word Search, Vol. II: Women in the Bible

COPYRIGHT © GIL PUBLICATIONS 2006

66. Peter's Mother-In-Law

AROSE	HOUSE	PETER
ARRIVED	ILL	PREPARED
BED	INLAW	SAW
BEGAN	INTO	SICK
COME	LAID	TOUCHED
FEVER	LEFT	UNTO
GOT	LYING	UP
HAND	MEAL	WAIT
HER	MINISTERED	WHEN
HIGH	MOTHER	WITH

GIL Publications, P. O. Box 80275, Brooklyn, NY 11208
www.BibleWordSearchPuzzles.com

67. Pheobe

Romans 16:1-2

I <u>commend</u> unto you <u>Phebe</u> our <u>sister</u>, which is a <u>servant</u> of the church which is at <u>Cenchrea</u>: That ye receive her in the Lord, as becometh saints, and that ye <u>assist</u> her in whatsoever <u>business</u> she hath need of you: for she hath been a <u>succourer</u> of many, and of myself also. (KJV)

I commend to you our sister <u>Phoebe</u>, a servant of the church in Cenchrea. I ask you to receive her in the Lord in a way <u>worthy</u> of the saints and to give her any help she may need from you, for she has been a <u>great</u> <u>help</u> to many people, including <u>me</u>. (NIV)

Our sister Phoebe, a <u>deacon</u> in the church in Cenchrea, will be coming to see you soon. Receive her in the Lord, as one who is worthy of high <u>honor</u>. Help her in every way you can, for she has helped <u>many</u> in their <u>needs</u>, including me.

Phoebe, a dear <u>Christian</u> <u>woman</u> from the <u>town</u> of Cenchreae, will be coming to see you soon. She has worked <u>hard</u> in the church there. Receive <u>her</u> as your sister in the Lord, giving her a <u>warm</u> Christian <u>welcome</u>. Help her in every way you can, for she has helped many in their needs, <u>including</u> me. (TLB)

I commend to you our sister Phoebe, who is a servant of the church which is at Cenchrea; that you <u>receive</u> her in the Lord in a <u>manner</u> worthy of the saints, and that you help her in whatever <u>matter</u> she may have need of you; for she herself has also been a helper of many, and of <u>myself</u> as <u>well</u>. (NASB)

Bible Word Search, Vol. II: Women in the Bible

COPYRIGHT © GIL PUBLICATIONS 2006

67. Pheobe

- ASSIST
- BUSINESS
- CENCHREA
- CHRISTIAN
- COMMEND
- DEACON
- GREAT
- HARD
- HELP
- HER
- HONOR
- INCLUDING
- MANNER
- MANY
- MATTER
- ME
- MYSELF
- NEEDS
- PHEBE
- PHEOBE
- RECEIVE
- SERVANT
- SISTER
- SUCCOURER
- TOWN
- WARM
- WELCOME
- WELL
- WOMAN
- WORTHY

68. Pilate's Wife

Matthew 27:19

While <u>Pilate</u> was <u>sitting</u> on the judge's <u>seat</u>, his <u>wife</u> <u>sent</u> him this <u>message</u>: "Don't have <u>anything</u> to do with that innocent man, for I have <u>suffered</u> a <u>great</u> <u>deal</u> <u>today</u> in a <u>dream</u> <u>because</u> of <u>him</u>." (NIV)

While he was sitting on the judgment seat, his wife sent him a message, saying, "Have <u>nothing</u> to do with that <u>righteous</u> Man; for last night I suffered greatly in a dream because of Him." (NLT)

Also, while he was seated on the judgment <u>bench</u>, his wife sent him a message, saying, Have nothing to do with that just and <u>upright</u> Man, for I have had a <u>painful</u> <u>experience</u> today in a dream because of Him. (AMP)

Just then, as Pilate was sitting on the judgment seat, his wife sent him this message: "<u>Leave</u> that <u>innocent</u> man <u>alone</u>, because I had a <u>terrible</u> <u>nightmare</u> about him <u>last</u> <u>night</u>." (NLT)

When he was <u>set</u> down on the judgment seat, his wife sent unto him, saying, Have thou nothing to do with that <u>just</u> man: for I have suffered <u>many</u> things this day in a dream because of him. (KJV)

68. Pilate's Wife

ALONE	JUST	RIGHTEOUS
ANYTHING	LAST	SEAT
BECAUSE	LEAVE	SENT
BENCH	MANY	SET
DEAL	MESSAGE	SITTING
DREAM	NIGHT	SUFFERED
EXPERIENCE	NIGHTMARE	TERRIBLE
GREAT	NOTHING	TODAY
HIM	PAINFUL	UPRIGHT
INNOCENT	PILATE	WIFE

69. Priscilla

After these things <u>Paul</u> departed from Athens, and came to <u>Corinth</u>; And found a certain Jew named <u>Aquila</u>, born in <u>Pontus</u>, lately come from <u>Italy</u>, with his wife <u>Priscilla</u>; (because that Claudius had commanded all Jews to depart from <u>Rome</u>) and came unto them.

And because he was of the same <u>craft</u>, he <u>abode</u> with them, and wrought: for by their <u>occupation</u> they were <u>tentmakers</u>. And he reasoned in the <u>synagogue</u> every <u>sabbath</u>, and persuaded the Jews and the Greeks.

And when Silas and Timotheus were come from Macedonia, Paul was <u>pressed</u> in the spirit, and testified to the Jews that Jesus was Christ.

… the Jews made insurrection with one <u>accord</u> against Paul, and brought him to the judgment seat, Saying, This <u>fellow</u> persuadeth men to worship God contrary to the <u>law</u>.

And Paul after this <u>tarried</u> there yet a good while, and then took his leave of the brethren, and <u>sailed</u> thence into <u>Syria</u>, and with him Priscilla and Aquila; having <u>shorn</u> his head in Cenchrea: for he had a <u>vow</u>.

And a certain Jew named <u>Apollos</u>, born at Alexandria, an eloquent man, and mighty in the scriptures, came to Ephesus.

This man was instructed in the way of the Lord; and being fervent in the spirit, he <u>spake</u> and taught diligently the things of the Lord, knowing only the baptism of John.

And he began to speak boldly in the synagogue: whom when Aquila and Priscilla had heard, they took him unto them, and <u>expounded</u> unto him the way of God more perfectly. (Acts 18:1-5, 12-13, 18, 24-26 KJV)

Greet Priscilla and Aquila my helpers in Christ Jesus: Who have for my life laid down their own <u>necks</u>: unto whom not only I give thanks, but also all the churches of the Gentiles. (Roman 16:3-4 KJV)

The churches of <u>Asia</u> salute you. Aquila and Priscilla <u>salute</u> you much in the Lord, with the church that is in their house. All the brethren greet you. <u>Greet</u> ye one another with an holy <u>kiss</u>. The salutation of me Paul with mine own hand. (1 Corinthians 16:19-21 KJV)

Bible Word Search, Vol. II: Women in the Bible

```
P X Q Z H P Z X E Z Y A C M Q
I T G S S N V M T A R R I E D
I T A L Y Z O E E L A W X S J
P X T G N R E I N F V P O L A
R L T B A R I R T C U G U V M
O U M M G D T A M A A A E E U
Q N A B O D E J A Y P Q T S Q
E F I R G R Z M K J O U A F O
D E D N U O P X E O L I C U F
B L E E E C V C R A L L O C P
M L S Y B C A Z S E O A R Z O
U O S S P A K E D W S J I S N
V W E U K Z I S S H O R N O T
N C R P R I S C I L L A T J U
H D P M Q Z S A B B A T H H S
```

COPYRIGHT © GIL PUBLICATIONS 2006

69. Priscilla

ABODE	ITALY	SABBATH
ACCORD	KISS	SAILED
APOLLOS	LAW	SALUTE
AQUILA	NECKS	SHORN
ASIA	OCCUPATION	SPAKE
CORINTH	PAUL	SYNAGOGUE
CRAFT	PONTUS	SYRIA
EXPOUNDED	PRESSED	TARRIED
FELLOW	PRISCILLA	TENTMAKERS
GREET	ROME	VOW

GIL Publications, P. O. Box 80275, Brooklyn, NY 11208
www.BibleWordSearchPuzzles.com

70. Salome, Mother of Zebedee's Children

Then came to him the mother of Zebedee's children with her sons, worshipping *him*, and desiring a certain thing of him. And he said unto her, What wilt thou? She saith unto him, Grant that these my two sons may sit, the one on thy right hand, and the other on the left, in thy kingdom. But Jesus answered and said, Ye know not what ye ask. Are ye able to drink of the cup that I shall drink of, and to be baptized with the baptism that I am baptized with? They say unto him, We are able. And he saith unto them, Ye shall drink indeed of my cup, and be baptized with the baptism that I am baptized with: but to sit on my right hand, and on my left, is not mine to give, but *it shall be given to them* for whom it is prepared of my Father. And when the ten heard *it*, they were moved with indignation against the two brethren. (Matthew 20:20-24 KJV)

Then Jesus uttered another loud cry and breathed his last. And the curtain in the Temple was torn in two, from top to bottom. When the Roman officer who stood facing him saw how he had died, he exclaimed, "Truly, this was the Son of God!"
Some women were there, watching from a distance, including Mary Magdalene, Mary (the mother of James the younger and of Joseph), and Salome.[1]They had been followers of Jesus and had cared for him while he was in Galilee. Then they and many other women had come with him to Jerusalem. (Mark 15:37-41 NLT)
When the Sabbath was over, Mary Magdalene, Mary the mother of James, and Salome bought spices so that they might go to anoint Jesus' body. Very early on the first day of the week, just after sunrise, they were on their way to the tomb and they asked each other, "Who will roll the stone away from the entrance of the tomb?"
But when they looked up, they saw that the stone, which was very large, had been rolled away.[5]As they entered the tomb, they saw a young man dressed in a white robe sitting on the right side, and they were alarmed.
"Don't be alarmed," he said. "You are looking for Jesus the Nazarene, who was crucified. He has risen! He is not here ..." (Mark 16:1-6 NIV)

Bible Word Search, Vol. II: Women in the Bible

70. Salome, Mother of Zebedee's Children

ABLE	FACING	NAZARENE
ANOINT	FATHER	RIGHT
CARED	FIRST	ROLLED
CHILDREN	GRANT	SIT
CUP	INDEED	SPICES
DRESSED	INDIGNATION	STONE
DRINK	KINGDOM	SUNRISE
EACH	LARGE	TOMB
EARLY	LEFT	WERE
ENTERED	MOVED	ZEBEDEE

71. Samaritan Women by Jacob's Well

So he came to a town in <u>Samaria</u> called Sychar, near the plot of ground Jacob had given to his son Joseph. Jacob's <u>well</u> was there, and Jesus, tired as he was from the <u>journey</u>, sat down by the well. It was about the sixth hour.

When a Samaritan woman came to draw water, Jesus said to her, "Will you give me a <u>drink</u>?" (His disciples had gone into the town to buy food.) The Samaritan woman said to him, "You are a <u>Jew</u> and I am a Samaritan woman. How can you ask me for a drink?" (For Jews do not <u>associate</u> with Samaritans.)

Jesus answered her, "If you knew the gift of God and who it is that asks you for a drink, you would have asked him and he would have given you <u>living water</u>."

"Sir," the woman said, "you have nothing to draw with and the well is <u>deep</u>. Where can you get this living water? Are you greater than our father Jacob, who gave us the well and drank from it himself, as did also his sons and his flocks and herds?"

Jesus answered, "Everyone who drinks this water will be <u>thirsty</u> again, but whoever drinks the water I give him will <u>never</u> thirst. Indeed, the water I give him will become in him a <u>spring</u> of water welling up to eternal life."

The woman said to him, "Sir, give me this water so that I won't get thirsty and have to keep coming here to draw water."

He told her, "Go, call your <u>husband</u> and come back."

"I have no husband," she <u>replied</u>.

Jesus said to her, "You are right when you say you have no husband. The fact is, you have had <u>five</u> husbands, and the man you now have is not your husband. What you have just said is quite <u>true</u>."

"Sir," the woman said, "I can see that you are a <u>prophet</u>. Our fathers worshiped on this <u>mountain</u>, but you Jews <u>claim</u> that the place where we must worship is in <u>Jerusalem</u>."

Jesus declared, "<u>Believe</u> me, woman, a <u>time</u> is coming when you will worship the Father neither on this mountain nor in Jerusalem. You Samaritans worship what you do not <u>know</u>; we worship what we do know, for <u>salvation</u> is from the Jews. Yet a time is coming and has now come when the true worshipers will worship the Father in <u>spirit</u> and <u>truth</u>, for they are the kind of worshipers the <u>Father</u> seeks. God is spirit, and his worshipers must worship in spirit and in truth."

The woman said, "I know that <u>Messiah</u>" (called <u>Christ</u>) "is coming. When he comes, he will explain everything to us."

Then Jesus declared, "I who speak to you <u>am</u> he." (John 4:4-26 NIV)

Bible Word Search, Vol. II: Women in the Bible

```
A M T R U E M B D W W T O F S
C H R I S T Y M R M E B A P M
B E L I E V E N I T J T I I T
S A L V A T I O N V H R A A H
N D C E C V W J K E I L O F I
I E M P H W S M R T C M N P R
A I N E V E R G J S H U U E S
T L W O N K M E B G P T P E T
N P C B R E R H Y C N R U D Y
U E Y E S U U Q U E C I I R D
O R T S S S F I V E N A V N T
M A I A B Y P L L E W R T I G
W A L A S A I R A M A S U K L
H E N P R O P H E T R N H O H
M D D T E T A I C O S S A W J
```

COPYRIGHT © GIL PUBLICATIONS 2006

71. Samarian Woman By Jacob's Well

AM	JERUSALEM	SALVATION
ASSOCIATE	JEW	SAMARIA
BELIEVE	JOURNEY	SPIRIT
CHRIST	KNOW	SPRING
CLAIM	LIVING	THIRSTY
DEEP	MESSIAH	TIME
DRINK	MOUNTAIN	TRUE
FATHER	NEVER	TRUTH
FIVE	PROPHET	WATER
HUSBAND	REPLIED	WELL

GIL Publications, P. O. Box 80275, Brooklyn, NY 11208
www.BibleWordSearchPuzzles.com

72. Sapphira, Ananias' Wife

But A certain man named <u>Ananias</u> with his wife <u>Sapphira</u> sold a <u>piece</u> of property,
And with his wife's <u>knowledge</u> and <u>connivance</u> he <u>kept</u> back and <u>wrongfully</u> <u>appropriated</u> some of the <u>proceeds</u>, bringing only a <u>part</u> and putting it at the feet of the <u>apostles</u>.
But Peter said, Ananias, why has <u>Satan</u> filled your <u>heart</u> that you should <u>lie</u> to and attempt to deceive the Holy Spirit, and should [in <u>violation</u> of your <u>promise</u>] withdraw secretly and appropriate to your own use part of the <u>price</u> from the <u>sale</u> of the land?
As <u>long</u> as it remained unsold, was it not still your own? And [even] after it was sold, was not [the <u>money</u>] at your disposal and under your control? Why then, is it that you have proposed and purposed in your heart to do this thing? [How could you have the heart to do such a deed?] You have not [simply] lied to men [playing <u>false</u> and showing yourself utterly <u>deceitful</u>] but to God.
Upon hearing these words, Ananias fell down and died. And great dread and terror took possession of all who heard of it. And the young men arose and wrapped up [the body] and carried it out and buried it.
Now after an <u>interval</u> of about three hours his wife came in, not having learned of what had happened.
And <u>Peter</u> said to her, Tell me, did you sell the land for so much? Yes, she said, for so much.
Then Peter said to her, How could you two have agreed and <u>conspired</u> together to try to <u>deceive</u> the Spirit of the Lord? Listen! The feet of those who have buried your husband are at the door, and they will <u>carry</u> you out [also].
And instantly she fell down at his feet and died; and the young men entering found her dead, and they carried her out and buried her beside her husband.
And the whole church and all others who heard of these things were appalled [great <u>awe</u> and strange <u>terror</u> and <u>dread</u> seized them]. (Acts 5:1-11 AMP)

Bible Word Search, Vol. II: Women in the Bible

```
T V A P I K Y U D R E T A A Y
V I R R J U E R P C O A P W V
S O I O A I E E N Z P R H E E
E L H M P A T A L P P O R S K
L A P I D E V U R T R I K E Z
T T P S R I F O R P O N E S T
S I A E N T P A F E C T V A S
O O S N I R E A L P E E I I P
P N O E I H L A I X E R E N R
A C C A Y S S E E Q D V C A I
U E T R E Y C N Q Y S A E N C
D E R G E E A P A R T L D A E
D A N N Q T E G D E L W O N K
C O O B A K D E R I P S N O C
L M B S W R O N G F U L L Y Y
```

Copyright © Gil Publications 2006

72. Sapphira

ANANIAS	FALSE	PIECE
APOSTLES	HEART	PRICE
APPROPRIATED	INTERVAL	PROCEEDS
AWE	KEPT	PROMISE
CARRY	KNOWLEDGE	SALE
CONNIVANCE	LIE	SAPPHIRA
CONSPIRED	LONG	SATAN
DECEITFUL	MONEY	TERROR
DECEIVE	PART	VIOLATION
DREAD	PETER	WRONGFULLY

GIL Publications, P. O. Box 80275, Brooklyn, NY 11208
www.BibleWordSearchPuzzles.com

73. Spiritual MotherHood

While Jesus was still talking to the <u>crowd</u>, his <u>mother</u> and <u>brothers</u> <u>stood</u> <u>outside</u>, <u>wanting</u> to speak to him. Someone told him, "Your mother and brothers are <u>standing</u> outside, wanting to speak to you."

He replied to him, "Who is my mother, and who are my brothers?" <u>Pointing</u> to his disciples, he said, "Here are my mother and my brothers. For whoever does the <u>will</u> of my Father in <u>heaven</u> is my brother and sister and mother." (Matthew 12:46-50 NIV)

Then Jesus' mother and brothers <u>arrived</u>. Standing outside, they <u>sent</u> <u>someone</u> in to <u>call</u> him. A crowd was sitting around him, and they told him, "Your mother and brothers are outside <u>looking</u> for you."

"Who are my mother and my brothers?" he <u>asked</u>.

Then he looked at <u>those</u> <u>seated</u> in a <u>circle</u> <u>around</u> him and said, "Here are my mother and my brothers! <u>Whoever</u> does God's will is my brother and <u>sister</u> and mother." (Mark 3:31-35 NIV)

Then came to him *his* mother and his brethren, and could not come at him for the <u>press</u>. And it was told him *by* <u>certain</u> which said, Thy mother and thy brethren stand without, <u>desiring</u> to see thee. And he <u>answered</u> and said unto them, My mother and my <u>brethren</u> are these <u>which</u> <u>hear</u> the <u>word</u> of God, and do it. (Luke 8:19-21 KJV)

Bible Word Search, Vol. II: Women in the Bible

73. Spiritual MotherHood

ANSWERED	DESIRING	SISTER
AROUND	HEAR	SOMEONE
ARRIVED	HEAVEN	STANDING
ASKED	LOOKING	STOOD
BRETHREN	MOTHER	THOSE
BROTHERS	OUTSIDE	WANTING
CALL	POINTING	WHICH
CERTAIN	PRESS	WHOEVER
CIRCLE	SEATED	WILL
CROWD	SENT	WORD

GIL Publications, P. O. Box 80275, Brooklyn, NY 11208
www.BibleWordSearchPuzzles.com

74. Ten Virgins

Then <u>shall</u> the <u>kingdom</u> of heaven be <u>likened</u> unto <u>ten</u> <u>virgins</u>, which took their lamps, and went forth to meet the <u>bridegroom</u>. And <u>five</u> of them were wise, and five *were* <u>foolish</u>. They that *were* foolish took their <u>lamps</u>, and took no <u>oil</u> with them: But the wise took oil in their <u>vessels</u> with their lamps. While the bridegroom <u>tarried</u>, they all <u>slumbered</u> and <u>slept</u>. And at <u>midnight</u> there was a <u>cry</u> made, Behold, the bridegroom <u>cometh</u>; go ye out to meet him. Then all those virgins <u>arose</u>, and <u>trimmed</u> their lamps. And the foolish said unto the wise, Give us of your oil; for our lamps are <u>gone</u> out. But the <u>wise</u> answered, saying, *Not so*; <u>lest</u> there be not enough for us and you: but go ye <u>rather</u> to them that sell, and buy for <u>yourselves</u>. And while they went to buy, the bridegroom came; and they that were ready went in with him to the marriage: and the <u>door</u> was <u>shut</u>. Afterward came also the other virgins, saying, Lord, Lord, open to us. But he answered and said, Verily I say unto you, I know you not. <u>Watch</u> therefore, for ye know <u>neither</u> the day nor the <u>hour</u> <u>wherein</u> the Son of man cometh. (Matthew 25:1-13 KJV)

Bible Word Search, Vol. II: Women in the Bible

74. Ten Virgins

AROSE	LAMPS	SLUMBERED
BRIDEGROOM	LEST	TARRIED
COMETH	LIKENED	TEN
CRY	MIDNIGHT	TRIMMED
DOOR	NEITHER	VESSELS
FIVE	OIL	VIRGINS
FOOLISH	RATHER	WATCH
GONE	SHALL	WHEREIN
HOUR	SHUT	WISE
KINGDOM	SLEPT	YOURSELVES

75. Widow Who Gave Two Mites

And Jesus sat over <u>against</u> the <u>treasury</u>, and <u>beheld</u> how the people <u>cast</u> <u>money</u> into the treasury: and many that were <u>rich</u> cast in <u>much</u>. And there came a <u>certain</u> <u>poor</u> <u>widow</u>, and she threw in <u>two</u> <u>mites</u>, which make a farthing. And he called *unto him* his <u>disciples</u>, and saith unto them, Verily I say unto you, That this poor widow hath cast <u>more</u> in, than all they which have cast into the treasury: For all *they* did cast in of their <u>abundance</u>; but she of her want did cast in all that she had, *even* all her <u>living</u>. (Mark 12:41-44 KJV)

As he looked up, Jesus saw the rich <u>putting</u> their <u>gifts</u> into the temple treasury. He also saw a poor widow put in two very <u>small</u> <u>copper</u> <u>coins</u>. "I tell you the truth," he said, "this poor widow has put in more than all the others. All these people gave their gifts out of their wealth; but she out of her <u>poverty</u> put in all she had to live on." (Luke 21:1-4 NIV)

While Jesus was in the <u>Temple</u>, he <u>watched</u> the rich people putting their gifts into the <u>collection</u> box. Then a poor widow came by and <u>dropped</u> in two <u>pennies</u>. "I assure you," he said, "this poor widow has given more than all the rest of them. For they have given a <u>tiny</u> part of their <u>surplus</u>, but she, poor as she is, has given <u>everything</u> she has." (Luke 21:1-4 NLT)

Bible Word Search, Vol. II: Women in the Bible

```
D I S C I P L E M T D X E W G
F Z U M C V H O Y T R E V O P
E Y L I V I N G H W O C E D Z
Z T P Z G E E C O P P E R I O
I R R T Y I U L G S P T Y W X
Q E U I P M F L P U E S T E N
E A S Q C E G T T M D S H O D
C S A N W H N S S Y E E I H T
N U B S I U D N Y Q Z T N L S
A R V E M O R E I X C I G Y N
D Y N K Q A C E H E A M N E I
N J A C P V L N L C S I N K A
U K P E A O O L P U T T I N G
B E H E L D O T O Y S A N J A
A O A X X C E R T A I N W G P
```

COPYRIGHT © GIL PUBLICATIONS 2006

75. Widows Who Gave Two Mites

ABUNDANCE	EVERYTHING	PUTTING
AGAINST	GIFTS	RICH
BEHELD	LIVING	SMALL
CAST	MITES	SURPLUS
CERTAIN	MONEY	TEMPLE
COINS	MORE	TINY
COLLECTION	MUCH	TREASURY
COPPER	PENNIES	TWO
DISCIPLE	POOR	WATCHED
DROPPED	POVERTY	WIDOW

GIL Publications, P. O. Box 80275, Brooklyn, NY 11208
www.BibleWordSearchPuzzles.com

76. Woman Caught In Adultery

Jesus returned to the <u>Mount</u> of <u>Olives</u>, but early the <u>next</u> <u>morning</u> he was back again at the <u>Temple</u>. A <u>crowd</u> soon <u>gathered</u>, and he sat down and <u>taught</u> them. As he was <u>speaking</u>, the teachers of <u>religious</u> <u>law</u> and <u>Pharisees</u> brought a woman they had <u>caught</u> in the act of <u>adultery</u>. They put her in front of the crowd.

"Teacher," they said to Jesus, "this woman was caught in the very act of adultery. The law of <u>Moses</u> says to <u>stone</u> her. What do you say?"

They were trying to <u>trap</u> him into saying something they could use against him, but Jesus stooped down and <u>wrote</u> in the dust with his <u>finger</u>. They kept demanding an answer, so he stood up again and said, "All right, stone her. But let those who have never sinned throw the first stones!" Then he stooped down again and wrote in the <u>dust</u>.

When the accusers heard this, they <u>slipped</u> <u>away</u> one by one, beginning with the oldest, until <u>only</u> Jesus was left in the <u>middle</u> of the crowd with the woman. Then Jesus <u>stood</u> up again and said to her, "Where are your <u>accusers</u>? Didn't even one of them <u>condemn</u> you?"

"No, Lord," she said.

And Jesus said, "Neither do I. Go and <u>sin</u> <u>no</u> <u>more</u>."

(John 8:1-11 NLT)

Bible Word Search, Vol. II: Women in the Bible

76. Woman Caught In Adultery

- ACCUSERS
- ADULTERY
- AWAY
- CAUGHT
- CONDEMN
- CROWD
- DUST
- FINGER
- GATHERED
- LAW
- MIDDLE
- MORE
- MORNING
- MOSES
- MOUNT
- NEXT
- NO
- OLIVES
- ONLY
- PHARISEES
- RELIGIOUS
- SIN
- SLIPPED
- SPEAKING
- STONE
- STOOD
- TAUGHT
- TEMPLE
- TRAP
- WROTE

77. Woman Who Begged For Daughter's Healing

Then Jesus went <u>thence</u>, and departed into the coasts of <u>Tyre</u> and <u>Sidon</u>. And, behold, a woman of <u>Canaan</u> came out of the same <u>coasts</u>, and cried unto him, saying, Have <u>mercy</u> on me, O Lord, <u>thou</u> Son of David; my daughter is <u>grievously</u> <u>vexed</u> with a <u>devil</u>. But he answered her not a word. And his disciples came and <u>besought</u> him, saying, Send her away; for she crieth after us. But he answered and said, I am not sent but unto the <u>lost</u> <u>sheep</u> of the house of <u>Israel</u>. Then came she and worshipped him, saying, Lord, help me. But he answered and said, It is not meet to take the children's bread, and to cast *it* to <u>dogs</u>. And she said, Truth, Lord: yet the dogs eat of the <u>crumbs</u> which fall from their <u>masters</u>' table. Then Jesus answered and said unto her, O woman, great *is* thy faith: be it unto thee even as thou <u>wilt</u>. And her daughter was made whole from that very hour. (Matthew 15:22-28 KJV)

Then Jesus left Galilee and went north to the region of Tyre. He tried to keep it <u>secret</u> that he was there, but he couldn't. As usual, the news of his arrival spread <u>fast</u>. Right away a woman came to him whose little girl was possessed by an evil spirit. She had heard about Jesus, and now she came and fell at his feet. She <u>begged</u> him to <u>release</u> her child from the demon's control.

Since she was a <u>Gentile</u>, born in <u>Syrian</u> <u>Phoenicia</u>, Jesus told her, "First I should help my own family, the Jews. It isn't <u>right</u> to take food from the children and <u>throw</u> it to the dogs."

She replied, "That's true, Lord, but even the dogs under the table are given some crumbs from the children's <u>plates</u>."

"Good answer!" he said. "And because you have answered so well, I have healed your daughter." And when she arrived home, her little <u>girl</u> was lying <u>quietly</u> in bed, and the demon was gone. (Mark 7:24-30 NLT)

Bible Word Search, Vol. II: Women in the Bible

```
W E M L E L I T N E G F C N P
M E R C Y X K E X I S R A E L
W I T Y P E S R B V U U A S A
G U Z Y T K M C Z M J J N I T
J T H G U O S E B G A D A D E
N A P S I A G S T H N Q N O S
V A D D H I U B A X A W L N A
E B I P H O E N I C I A U Q E
X Y W F B E G G E D R Y M U L
E G R I E V O U S L Y M Z I E
D I G E C N E H T T S I D E R
L D T K T R H D D H H A E T T
C O A S T S X E L R E G V L H
I G S O C H A F U O E M I Y O
O S Q T G L Q M V W P W L R U
```

COPYRIGHT © GIL PUBLICATIONS 2006

77. Woman Who Begged for Daughter's Healing

BEGGED	GRIEVOUSLY	SECRET
BESOUGHT	ISRAEL	SHEEP
CAANAN	LOST	SIDON
COASTS	MASTER	SYRIAN
CRUMBS	MERCY	THENCE
DEVIL	PHOENICIA	THOU
DOGS	PLATES	THROW
FAST	QUIETLY	TYRE
GENTILE	RELEASE	VEXED
GIRL	RIGHT	WILT

GIL Publications, P. O. Box 80275, Brooklyn, NY 11208
www.BibleWordSearchPuzzles.com

78. Woman With the Issue of Blood

And a certain woman, which had an issue of blood twelve years,
And had suffered many things of many physicians, and had spent all that she had, and was nothing bettered, but rather grew worse,
When she had heard of Jesus, came in the press behind, and touched his garment.
For she said, If I may touch but his clothes, I shall be whole.
And straightway the fountain of her blood was dried up; and she felt in her body that she was healed of that plague.
And Jesus, immediately knowing in himself that virtue had gone out of him, turned him about in the press, and said, Who touched my clothes?
And his disciples said unto him, Thou seest the multitude thronging thee, and sayest thou, Who touched me?
And he looked round about to see her that had done this thing.
But the woman fearing and trembling, knowing what was done in her, came and fell down before him, and told him all the truth.
And he said unto her, Daughter, thy faith hath made thee whole; go in peace, and be whole of thy plague. (Mark 5:25-34 KJV)

Bible Word Search, Vol. II: Women in the Bible

78. Woman With the Issue of Blood

BEHIND	GONE	THRONGING
BETTERED	HEARD	TOLD
BLOOD	ISSUE	TOUCH
CERTAIN	MULTITUDE	TREMBLING
CLOTHES	PHYSICIANS	TWELVE
DRIED	PLAGUE	UP
FAITH	PRESS	VIRTUE
FELL	SEEST	WHOLE
FOUNTAIN	SPENT	WORSE
GARMENT	SUFFERED	YEARS

GIL Publications, P. O. Box 80275, Brooklyn, NY 11208
www.BibleWordSearchPuzzles.com

79. Women in Church

And I want women to be <u>modest</u> in their <u>appearance</u>. They should <u>wear</u> <u>decent</u> and <u>appropriate</u> clothing and not <u>draw</u> attention to themselves by the way they <u>fix</u> their <u>hair</u> or by wearing gold or <u>pearls</u> or expensive clothes. [10]For women who claim to be <u>devoted</u> to God should make <u>themselves</u> <u>attractive</u> by the <u>good</u> things they do. (2 Timothy 2:9:-10 NLT)

Let the woman <u>learn</u> in <u>silence</u> with all <u>subjection</u>. [12]But I <u>suffer</u> not a woman to teach, nor to <u>usurp</u> authority over the man, but to be in silence. [13]For Adam was first formed, then Eve. [14]And Adam was not deceived, but the woman being deceived was in the transgression. [15]Notwithstanding she shall be saved in <u>child</u>-<u>bearing</u>, if they continue in <u>faith</u> and <u>charity</u> and <u>holiness</u> with <u>sobriety</u>. (1 Timothy 2:11-15 KJV)

As in all the <u>congregations</u> of the saints, [34]women should <u>remain</u> silent in the churches. They are not allowed to <u>speak</u>, but must be in submission, as the Law says. [35]If they want to <u>inquire</u> about something, they should ask their own husbands at <u>home</u>; for it is disgraceful for a <u>woman</u> to speak in the church. (1 Corinthians 14:33-35 NIV)

Bible Word Search, Vol. II: Women in the Bible

79. Women in Church

APPEARANCE	FAITH	REMAIN
APPROPRIATE	FIX	SILENCE
ATTRACTIVE	GOOD	SOBRIETY
BEARING	HAIR	SPEAK
CHARITY	HOLINESS	SUBJECTION
CHILD	HOME	SUFFER
CONGREGATIONS	INQUIRE	THEMSELVES
DECENT	LEARN	USURP
DEVOTED	MODEST	WEAR
DRAW	PEARLS	WOMAN

GIL Publications, P. O. Box 80275, Brooklyn, NY 11208
www.BibleWordSearchPuzzles.com

80. Women With Jesus

Not long <u>afterward</u> Jesus began a tour of the <u>nearby</u> <u>cities</u> and villages to <u>announce</u> the <u>Good</u> <u>News</u> concerning the Kingdom of God. He took his twelve disciples with him, along with some women he had healed and from whom he had <u>cast</u> out evil spirits. Among them were Mary Magdalene, from whom he had cast out <u>seven</u> <u>demons</u>; <u>Joanna</u>, the wife of <u>Chuza</u>, Herod's <u>business</u> manager; <u>Susanna</u>; and many others who were <u>contributing</u> from their own <u>resources</u> to <u>support</u> Jesus and his disciples. (Luke 8:1-3 NLT)

The women who had come with Jesus from <u>Galilee</u> followed Joseph and saw the <u>tomb</u> and how his body was laid in it. Then they went home and prepared <u>spices</u> and <u>perfumes</u>. But they <u>rested</u> on the Sabbath in <u>obedience</u> to the commandment. (Luke 23:55-56 NIV)

Near the cross of Jesus stood his mother, his mother's sister, Mary the wife of Clopas, and Mary Magdalene. (John 19:25 NIV)

Some women were <u>watching</u> from a <u>distance</u>. Among them were Mary Magdalene, Mary the mother of James the younger and of Joses, and <u>Salome</u>. [1]In Galilee these women had followed him and cared for his needs. Many other women who had come up with him to Jerusalem were also there. (Mark 15:40-41 NIV)

Now upon the first *day* of the week, very early in the morning, they came unto the <u>sepulchre</u>, bringing the spices which they had prepared, and certain *others* with them. And they found the stone rolled away from the sepulchre. And they entered in, and found not the body of the Lord Jesus ... And they <u>remembered</u> his words, And returned from the sepulchre, and told all these things unto the <u>eleven</u>, and to all the rest. It was Mary Magdalene, and Joanna, and Mary *the mother* of James, and other *women that were* with them, which told these things unto the apostles ... And it came to pass, that, while they communed *together* and <u>reasoned</u>, Jesus himself drew near, and went with them ... And the one of them, whose name was <u>Cleopas</u>, answering said unto him, Art thou only a stranger in Jerusalem, and hast not known the things which are come to pass there in these days ... Then he said unto them, O fools, and slow of heart to believe all that the prophets have spoken: Ought not Christ to have suffered these things, and to enter into his glory ... And their eyes were opened, and they knew him ... (Luke 24:13, 8-10, 18, 25-26, 31 KJV)

Bible Word Search, Vol. II: Women in the Bible

80. Women With Jesus

- AFTERWARD
- ANNOUNCE
- BUSINESS
- CAST
- CHUZA
- CITIES
- CLEOPAS
- CONTRIBUTING
- DEMONS
- DISTANCE
- ELEVEN
- GALILEE
- GOOD
- JOANNA
- NEARBY
- NEWS
- OBEDIENCE
- PERFUMES
- REASONED
- REMEMBERED
- RESOURCES
- RESTED
- SALOME
- SEPULCHRE
- SEVEN
- SPICES
- SUPPORT
- SUSANNA
- TOMB
- WATCHING

GIL Publications, P. O. Box 80275, Brooklyn, NY 11208
www.BibleWordSearchPuzzles.com

81. Aged and Young Women

Titus 2:1-5

But speak thou the things which become <u>sound</u> <u>doctrine</u>: That the aged men be <u>sober</u>, <u>grave</u>, <u>temperate</u>, sound in faith, in charity, in patience. The <u>aged</u> women <u>likewise</u>, that *they be* in <u>behavior</u> as becometh holiness, not <u>false</u> <u>accusers</u>, not given to much <u>wine</u>, teachers of good things; That they may teach the young women to be sober, to love their husbands, to love their children, *To be* <u>discreet</u>, <u>chaste</u>, <u>keepers</u> at home, good, <u>obedient</u> to their own husbands, that the word of God be not <u>blasphemed</u>. (KJV)

You must teach what is in accord with sound doctrine. Teach the older men to be temperate, worthy of <u>respect</u>, self-<u>controlled</u>, and sound in faith, in <u>love</u> and in <u>endurance</u>.

Likewise, teach the older women to be <u>reverent</u> in the way they live, not to be <u>slanderers</u> or addicted to much wine, but to teach what is good. Then they can train the younger women to love their husbands and children, to be self-controlled and pure, to be busy at home, to be kind, and to be <u>subject</u> to their husbands, so that no one will <u>malign</u> the word of God. (NIV)

But as for you, <u>promote</u> the kind of living that reflects right teaching. Teach the older men to exercise self-control, to be worthy of respect, and to live wisely. They must have strong faith and be filled with love and patience.

Similarly, teach the older women to live in a way that is <u>appropriate</u> for someone serving the Lord. They must not go around speaking evil of others and must not be <u>heavy</u> <u>drinkers</u>. Instead, they should teach others what is good. These older women must <u>train</u> the younger women to love their husbands and their children, to live <u>wisely</u> and be pure, to take care of their homes, to do good, and to be submissive to their husbands. Then they will not bring shame on the word of God. (NLT)

Bible Word Search, Vol. II: Women in the Bible

81. Aged and Young Women

ACCUSERS	ENDURANCE	RESPECT
AGED	FALSE	REVERENT
APPROPRIATE	GRAVE	SLANDERERS
BEHAVIOR	HEAVY	SOBER
BLASPHEMED	KEEPERS	SOUND
CHASTE	LIKEWISE	SUBJECT
CONTROLLED	LOVE	TEMPERATE
DISCREET	MALIGN	TRAIN
DOCTRINE	OBEDIENT	WINE
DRINKERS	PROMOTE	WISELY

GIL Publications, P. O. Box 80275, Brooklyn, NY 11208
www.BibleWordSearchPuzzles.com

82. Widows and Idle Women

   Rebuke not an elder, but entreat him as a father; *and* the younger men as brethren; The elder women as mothers; the younger as sisters, with all purity.
   Honour widows that are widows indeed. But if any widow have children or nephews, let them learn first to show piety at home, and to requite their parents: for that is good and acceptable before God. Now she that is a widow indeed, and desolate, trusteth in God, and continueth in supplications and prayers night and day. But she that liveth in pleasure is dead while she liveth. And these things give in charge, that they may be blameless. But if any provide not for his own, and specially for those of his own house, he hath denied the faith, and is worse than an infidel. Let not a widow be taken into the number under threescore years old, having been the wife of one man, Well reported of for good works; if she have brought up children, if she have lodged strangers, if she have washed the saints' feet, if she have relieved the afflicted, if she have diligently followed every good work. But the younger widows refuse: for when they have begun to wax wanton against Christ, they will marry; Having damnation, because they have cast off their first faith. And withal they learn *to be* idle, wandering about from house to house; and not only idle, but tattlers also and busybodies, speaking things which they ought not. I will therefore that the younger women marry, bear children, guide the house, give none occasion to the adversary to speak reproachfully. For some are already turned aside after Satan. If any man or woman that believeth have widows, let them relieve them, and let not the church be charged; that it may relieve them that are widows indeed. (1 Timothy 5:1-16 KJV)

Bible Word Search, Vol. II: Women in the Bible

```
D A M N A T I O N Y T I R U P
E E L D I Q S W E H P E N A W
S Y W S E I D O B Y S U B A I
O J I J L N L R D M N J X U D
L E D I F N I S E G O O C D O
A W I Q T A O E G Q I J E I W
T E L I H W U L D D T S K L S
E T T W R L F B O E A S U I F
T A A D E R E A L T C E B G E
I T E Y E N T E C I L E E V
U T R T S G O P G I L E R N E
Q L T E C N T E R L P M E T I
E E N I O U N C A F P A D L L
R R E P R O A C H F U L L Y E
E S O G E Y W A C A S B E S R
```

COPYRIGHT © GIL PUBLICATIONS 2006

82. Widows and Idle Women

ACCEPTABLE	ENTREAT	REQUITE
AFFLICTED	IDLE	SUPPLICATIONS
BLAMELESS	INFIDEL	TATTLERS
BUSYBODIES	LODGED	THREESCORE
CHARGE	NEPHEWS	WANTON
DAMNATION	PIETY	WAX
DENIED	PURITY	WIDOWS
DESOLATE	REBUKE	WHILE
DILIGENTLY	RELIEVE	WORSE
ELDER	REPROACHFULLY	YOUNGER

GIL Publications, P. O. Box 80275, Brooklyn, NY 11208
www.BibleWordSearchPuzzles.com

Bible Word Search, Vol. II: Women in the Bible

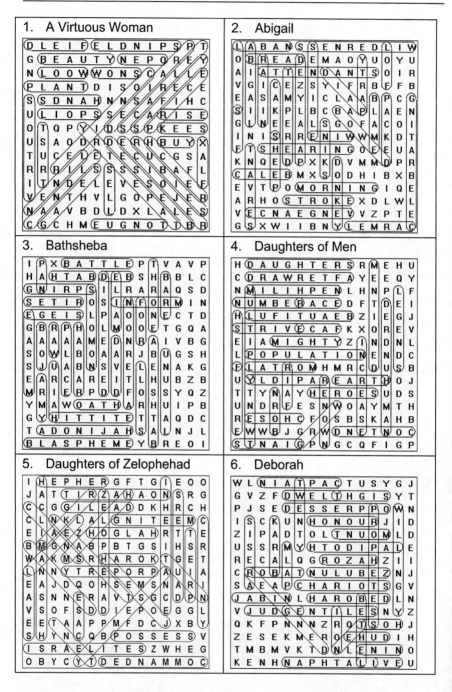

GIL Publications, P. O. Box 80275, Brooklyn, NY 11208
www.BibleWordSearchPuzzles.com

Bible Word Search, Vol. II: Women in the Bible

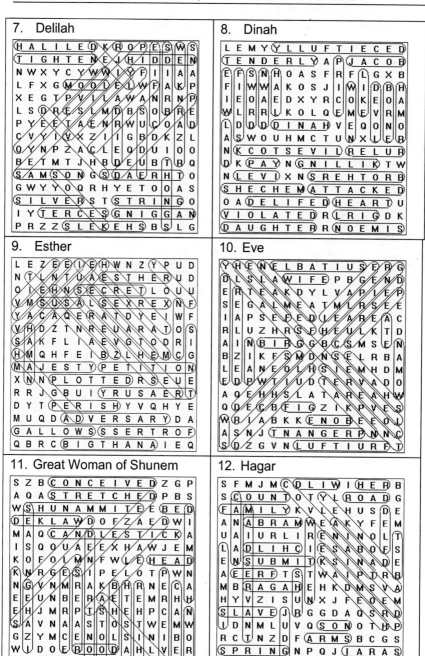

GIL Publications, P. O. Box 80275, Brooklyn, NY 11208
www.BibleWordSearchPuzzles.com

Bible Word Search, Vol. II: Women in the Bible

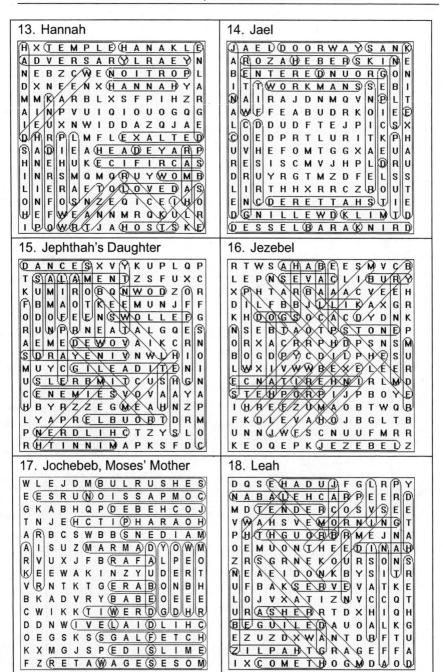

Bible Word Search, Vol. II: Women in the Bible

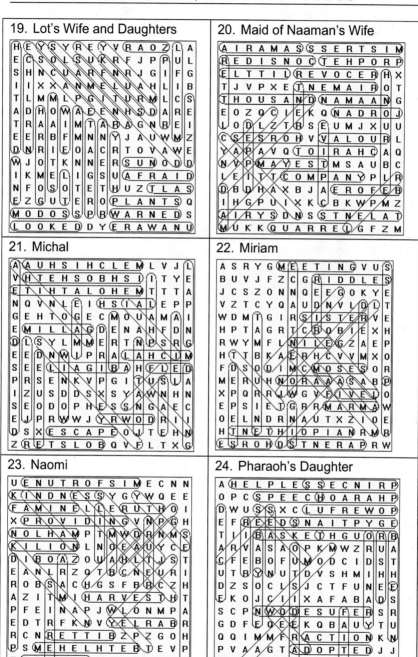

GIL Publications, P. O. Box 80275, Brooklyn, NY 11208
www.BibleWordSearchPuzzles.com

Bible Word Search, Vol. II: Women in the Bible

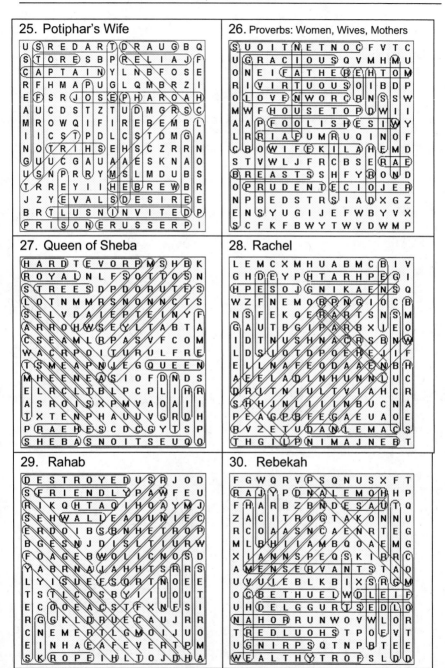

Bible Word Search, Vol. II: Women in the Bible

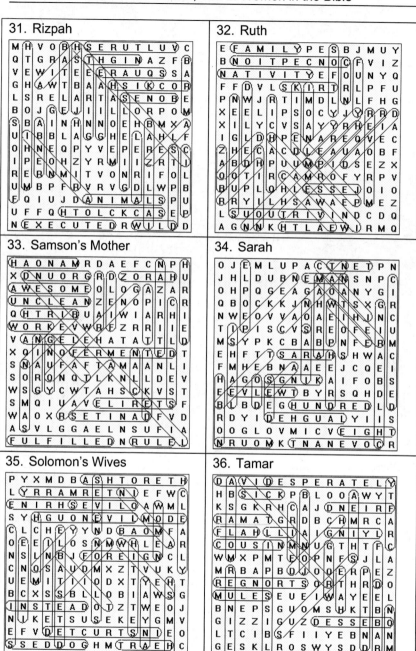

Bible Word Search, Vol. II: Women in the Bible

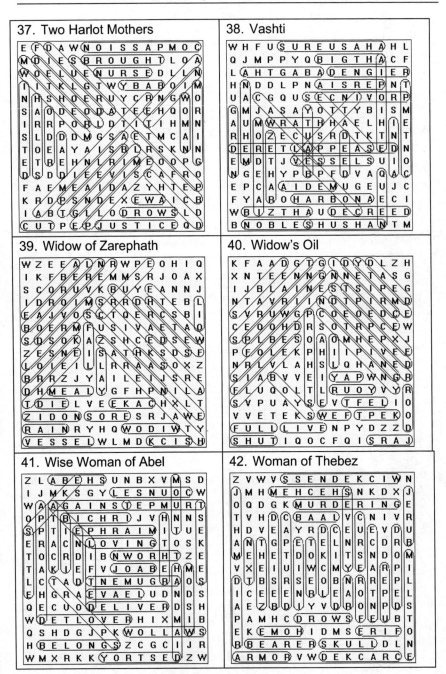

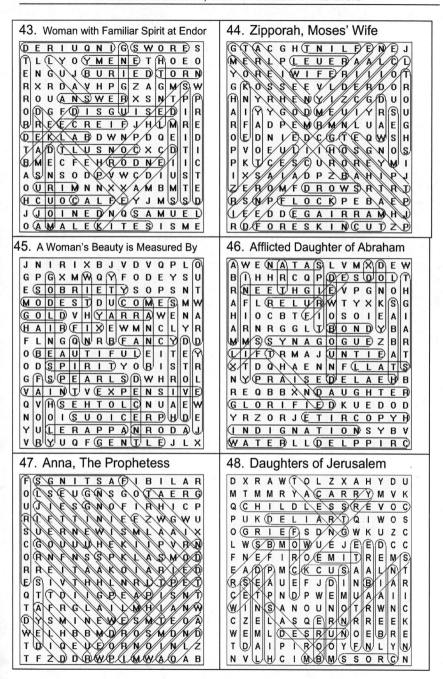

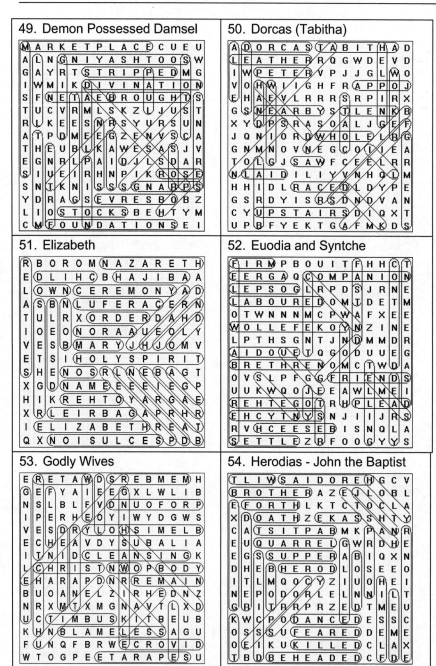

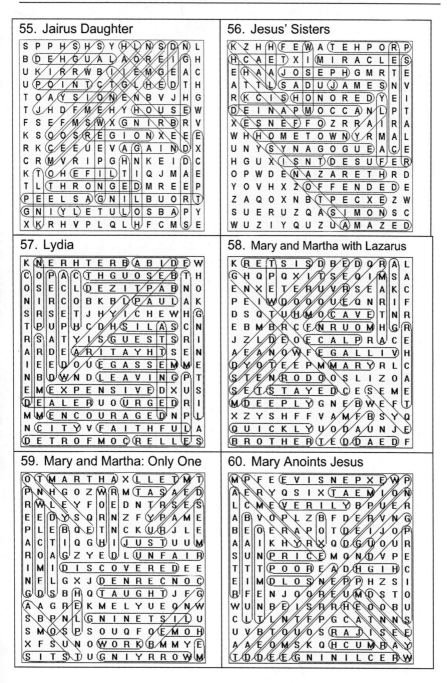

Bible Word Search, Vol. II: Women in the Bible

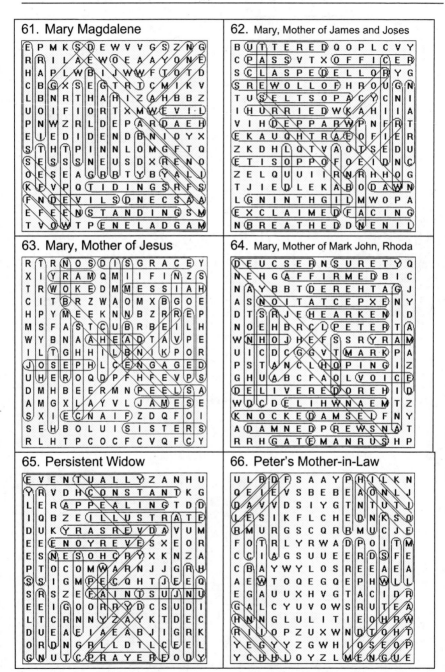

Bible Word Search, Vol. II: Women in the Bible

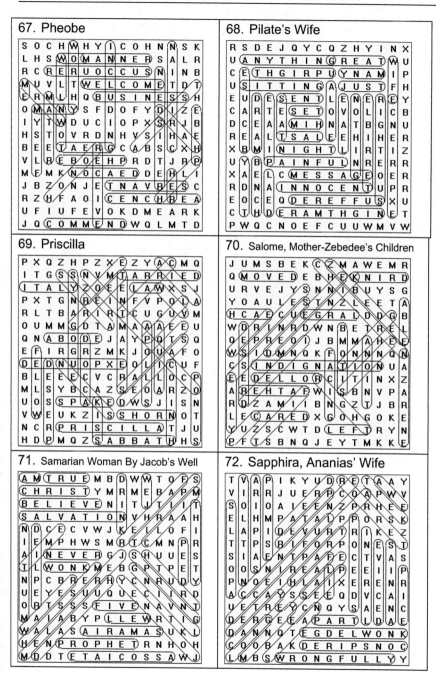

Bible Word Search, Vol. II: Women in the Bible

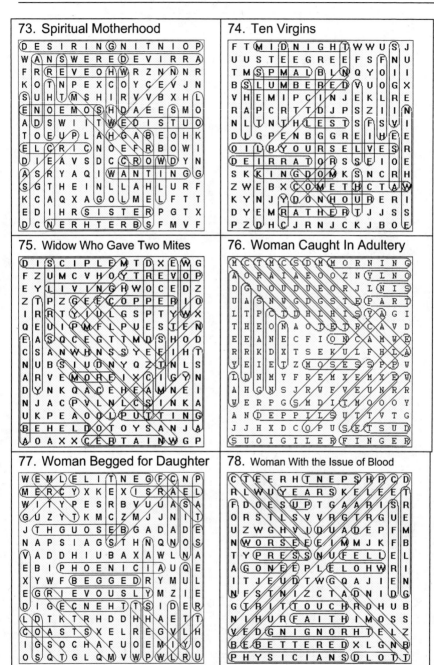

Bible Word Search, Vol. II: Women in the Bible

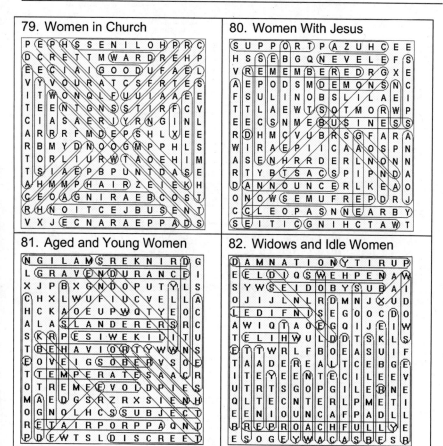

Do You Have a Relationship With God?

The Bible tells us that:

> ... if you confess with your mouth, "Jesus is Lord," and believe in your heart that God raised him from the dead, you will be saved.
>
> Romans 10:9 KJV

Have You Accepted Jesus as Your Lord?

If you do not have a relationship with God – through accepting Jesus as Lord – then I invite you to pray the following prayer:

> Lord, I come before you today to confess that I accept Jesus as my Lord and Savior and that I believe you raised Him from the dead. I believe that He died for my sins and that only through Him can I be saved.
>
> Lord, please forgive me of all my sins and accept me into your kingdom. Lord, I welcome the Holy Spirit into my heart today.
>
> I thank you Lord. In Jesus' Name, Amen.

As a born-again Christian you can best maintain your walk with God by attending a Bible teaching church, studying and reading God's Word daily, praying continuously and fellowshipping with other serious Christians. A good place to start your Bible reading is with the book/gospel of John. If you have questions or need help please write to me at:

Akili Kumasi, GIL Publications
P.O. Box 80275, Brooklyn, NY 11208
or
prayer@gilpublications.com

Books Available from
GIL PUBLICATIONS.COM

Bible Word Search Book Series

Bible Word Search, Vo. I: *Bible Extracts and Puzzles*
PRICE: $7.95 - ISBN-13: 978-0-9626035-0-1
- Enjoy this Great way to start with God's Word
- 80 different puzzle themes - help you to know the Bible
- Helps you find 100's of popular Bible verses
- Have fun with "Word" puzzle and develop in God's Word at the same time

Bible Word Search, Volume II: *Women in the Bible*
PRICE: $7.95 - ISBN-13: 978-0-9626035-3-2
- Encourage women and girls with fun puzzle/activities about women
- Be knowledgeable of all the Women in Biblical history
- Details about women in the Bible at your finger tips
- Challenging puzzles - lots of fun for everyone

Bible Word Search, Volume III: *Fathers in the Bible*
PRICE: $7.95 - ISBN-13: 978-0-9626035-4-9
- Work puzzles that emphasize the power and love of God the Father
- The Biblical fathers were – good & bad
- 80 puzzles mean fun and games while learning
- Great fun with puzzles - great information with scriptures

GIL Publications, P. O. Box 80275, Brooklyn, NY 11208
www.BibleWordSearchPuzzles.com

Bible Word Search, Vol. II: Women in the Bible

Bible Word Search, Volume IV: *Prayers in the Bible*
PRICE: $7.95 - ISBN-13: 978-0-9626035-2-5
- Work puzzles that emphasize the power of prayer
- 80 puzzles means fun and games while learning
- Show you how to pray, lessons & examples of prayers
- Great stories of victorious prayer warriors from the Bible

Bible Word Search, Volume V: *Victories in the Bible*
PRICE: $7.95 - ISBN-13: 978-0-9626035-8-7
- Work puzzles that emphasize God-given Victories
- 80 puzzles means fun and games while learning
- Puzzles show how God defeated many enemies in the Bible
- Great stories of OverComers and Divine Intervention

Forthcoming:

Volume VI:	**Parables in the Bible**
Volume VII:	**Promises in the Bible**
Volume VIII:	**Miracles and Healings**
Volume IX:	**God Speaks in the Bible**
Volume X:	**Traitors in the Bible**
Volume IX:	**OverComers in the Bible**

GIL PUBLICATIONS
has a new website dedicated to the
Bible Word Search Book Series
www.BibleWordSearchPuzzles.com

GIL Publications, P. O. Box 80275, Brooklyn, NY 11208
www.BibleWordSearchPuzzles.com

Bible Word Search, Vol. II: Women in the Bible

101 In the Bible Book Series

101 Women in the Bible:
Bible Scriptures & Biblical Lessons
PRICE: $7.95 - ISBN-13: 978-0-9626035-6-3
- Biblical Lessons from over 100 women in the Bible
- Documented stories of heroines and villainesses
- Easy research at your fingertips
- Learn the Bible - read about women in Biblical times

101 Prayers in the Bible:
Bible Scriptures and Biblical Lessons
PRICE: $7.95 - ISBN-13: 978-0-9626035-7-0
- A compilation of over 100 prayers in the Bible
- Bible Study Article on the Power of Prayer
- Learn God's instructions for praying
- Biblical Lessons on How to Pray from the Bible

101 Victories in the Bible
Bible Scriptures and Biblical Lessons
PRICE: $7.95 - ISBN-13: 978-0-9626035-7-0
- A compilation over 100 victories in the Bible
- Bible Study Article on The Battle is the Lord's
- Learn God's instructions for being an OverComer
- Biblical Lessons on winning and conquering

GIL Publications, P. O. Box 80275, Brooklyn, NY 11208
www.BibleWordSearchPuzzles.com

FatherHood Book Series

Fun Meals for Fathers and Sons
Recipes & Activities for Bonding & Mentoring
PRICE: $7.95 - ISBN-13: 978-0-9626035-1-8
- Cook up some fond memories
- easy recipes-fun activities
- Need help in fathering - here's some food for thought!
- Bond with your children – easy over a Fun Meal

On the Outside Looking In: *Hope for Separated Fathers Who Want To Be Good Fathers*
PRICE: $7.95 - ISBN-13: 978-0-9626035-5-6
- Gain strategies for making FatherHood work
- Use 7 Principles of Good FatherHood to train children
- Be informed - issues facing divorced & absent fathers
- Gain cooperation from children's mother

Bible Word Search, Volume III: *Fathers in the Bible*
PRICE: $7.95 - ISBN-13: 978-0-9626035-4-9
- Work puzzles that emphasize the power and love of God the Father
- The Biblical fathers – good and bad
- 80 puzzles mean fun and games while learning
- Great fun with puzzles - great information with scriptures

GIL Publications, P. O. Box 80275, Brooklyn, NY 11208
www.BibleWordSearchPuzzles.com

Bible Word Search, Vol. II: Women in the Bible

Women In the Bible Book Series

Bible Word Search, Volume II: *Women in the Bible*
PRICE: $7.95 - ISBN-13: 978-0-9626035-3-2
- Encourage women and girls with fun puzzle/activities about women
- Be knowledgeable of all the Women in Biblical history
- Details about women in the Bible at your finger tips
- Challenging puzzles - lots of fun for everyone

101 Women in the Bible:
Bible Scriptures & Biblical Lessons
PRICE: $7.95 - ISBN-13: 978-0-9626035-6-3
- Biblical Lessons from over 100 women in the Bible
- Documented stories of heroines and villainesses
- Easy research at your fingertips
- Learn the Bible by reading about women in Biblical times

GIL Publications, P. O. Box 80275, Brooklyn, NY 11208
www.BibleWordSearchPuzzles.com

GIL PUBLICATIONS.com
Quick Order Form

Mail Order.................... Gil Publications
P. O. Box 80275, Brooklyn, NY 11208
Telephone Orders .... (718) 386-6434
Website Orders .... www.GILpublications.com
E-Mail Orders .... orders@GILpublications.com

Book Title	Price	Qty/#	Total
Bible Word Search Book Series			
Vol. I: Bible Extracts and Puzzles	$7.95		
Vol. II: Women in the Bible	$7.95		
Vol. III: Fathers in the Bible	$7.95		
Vol. IV: Prayers in the Bible	$7.95		
Vol. IV: Victories in the Bible	$7.95		
101 In the Bible Book Series			
101 Women in the Bible	$7.95		
101 Prayers in the Bible	$7.95		
101 Victories in the Bible	$7.95		
FatherHood Book Series			
Fun Meals for Fathers and Sons	$7.95		
On the Outside Looking In	$7.95		
		Sub-Total	
	NY Residents Add ___% Tax		
	Shipping ($2.00 1st book, $1.00 each additional)		
	(Buy 4 – Get 1 Free)	Total	

Payment: ☐ Check   ☐ Money Order
Name:_____
Address:_____
City:_____ State:_____ Zip:_____
Telephone:_____
E-Mail:_____

To pay by Credit or Debit Card – go to our website
www.GILpublications.com

GIL Publications, P. O. Box 80275, Brooklyn, NY 11208
www.BibleWordSearchPuzzles.com

Bible Word Search, Vol. II: Women In the Bible

"We OverCome Through the Power of God's Love!"

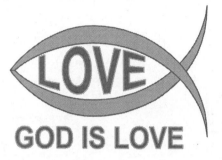

Send e-mail address to GIL Publications

to

Receive FREE Bible Word Search Puzzles and Bible Study Articles

GIL PUBLICATIONS.com
THE GOD IS LOVE MINISTRIES
P. O. Box 80275
Brooklyn, New York 11208
www.GILpublications.com

info@GILpublications.com

GIL Publications, P. O. Box 80275, Brooklyn, NY 11208
www.BibleWordSearchPuzzles.com